OBRONI

AND THE CHOCOLATE FACTORY

*An Unlikely Story of Globalization
and Ghana's First Gourmet Chocolate Bar*

STEVEN WALLACE

Skyhorse Publishing

Skyhorse Publishing books may be purchased in bulk at special discounts for sales promotion, corporate gifts, fund-raising, or educational purposes. Special editions can also be created to specifications. For details, contact the Special Sales Department, Skyhorse Publishing, 307 West 36th Street, 11th Floor, New York, NY 10018 or info@ skyhorsepublishing.com.

Skyhorse® and Skyhorse Publishing® are registered trademarks of Skyhorse Publishing, Inc.®, a Delaware corporation.

Visit our website at www.skyhorsepublishing.com.

10 9 8 7 6 5 4 3 2 1

Library of Congress Cataloging-in-Publication Data

Names: Wallace, Steven, author.
Title: Obroni and the chocolate factory : an unlikely story of globalization
   and Ghana's first gourmet chocolate bar / Steven Wallace.
Description: New York City : Skyhorse Publishing, 2017.
Identifiers: LCCN 2017034447 (print) | LCCN 2017037005 (ebook) | ISBN
   9781510723665 (ebook) | ISBN 9781510723658 (hardcover : alk. paper)
Subjects: LCSH: Omanhene Cocoa Bean Company--History. | Chocolate
   industry--Ghana. | Ghana--Economic conditions--20th century. |
   Ghana--Economic conditions--21st century.
Classification: LCC HD9200.G42 (ebook) | LCC HD9200.G42 W35 2017 (print) |
   DDC 338.1737409667--dc23
LC record available at https://lccn.loc.gov/2017034447

Cover design by Erin Seaward-Hiatt
Cover photo by iStock

Printed in the United States of America

To Linda B., whose steadfast belief and mirific support
defy any rational expectation.

And to the people of the Republic of Ghana,
who, in ways both modest and magnificent,
taught me most of life's important lessons.
This book is an expression of my deep affection
for your remarkable country.

Contents

Acknowledgments

A company twenty-six years in the making owes a prodigious debt to a great many individuals who shared what the Irish call the gift of second sight. They saw the future—or at least they bought into the future that I described. Their enthusiasm buoyed my spirits and lit my path. To those who bought the first production run of Omanhene chocolate, I could hug each and every one of you.

My love to the families of Professor Ansre of the language department at the University of Ghana-Legon, Yaw Brobbey, and Shafik and Ethel Natafgi, who so readily and graciously opened their hearts and homes to their *obroni* son.

To the volunteers and staff of AFS Intercultural Programs, AFS-USA, and AFS-Ghana for making the world a smaller, safer, and better place. Special thanks to AFSers Mrs. Gladys Osae-Addo, Reverend Setriakor Nyomi, Anne Ebert, and Suzanne Kessler.

To my brother Jonathan Wallace and sister-in-law Ruth Wallace, whose unwavering support and loyalty to the cause is the stuff of legend.

To Kojo Afedzi Hayford and Joyce Hayford, who opened their home and hearts to me; no matter how the Omanhene story ends, having you as a part of my life will have made it all worthwhile.

To Michael Caughlin, Daniel Gyimah, Flt. Lt. Joseph Atiemo (Ret.), Mr. K. B. Simpson, Jeffrey Frank, Ruth Lebed, John Timson, Isaac Osei, William Mensah, Cecilia Dapaah, Hannah Tetteh, Kyeretwie Opoku, Leslie Amissah, Carol Castiel, and Stephanie Zonis, who believed when there was precious little reason to do so.

To Oggie Kim and Anna Leider, who were present at the debut in New York City providing invaluable help at the Fancy Food Show in 1994.

To Peter Krupp and Jeffrey Leavell, who jumped in early and remained steadfastly loyal throughout. To Takeo and Cha Cha Mogami, who brought Omanhene to Japan. To Tony Weber, Bonnie Wolfe, and Judy Alexander.

To David and Maryclare Greif and Scot and Carolyn Trojanowski.

To the many chefs who generously shared their talents with me, often allowing me to work shoulder to shoulder with them in kitchens across the world, Christine McCabe, David Rexford, Peter Sandroni, Sandra Suria, and David Swanson.

To Peter Tichansky and his colleagues at BCIU, the Business Council for International Understanding, and to Franklin Kennedy and the Corporate Council on Africa for courtesies extended at the very beginning of my journey, when I had precious little to contribute to their fine organizations.

To Professors Anani Dzidzienyo, Pat McHugh, and Barrett Hazeltine. To J. Brian Atwood, Alan Harlam, Lizzie Pollack, and Liz Malone.

I count myself lucky indeed to be working with the remarkable Chef François Kwaku-Dongo, whose friendship, optimism, and enthusiasm have forever changed the way I view the world.

To the members of the US Foreign Service, US State Department, US Department of Commerce, Foreign Agriculture Service, US Trade and Development Agency, USAID, and Peace Corps, whose record of service seems to me underappreciated and often misunderstood by many of us at home. These public servants possess impressive language and cross-cultural skills, keen intellects, and unstinting hearts; they do our country proud and represent, for many around the globe, their first and only contact with the United States.

A most heartfelt debt of gratitude to William V. Madison, an extraordinary writer whose prose often compels one to stop and take a breath; he is a perspicacious editor and man of deep sensitivity, generosity, and kindness. Bill first saw the potential of this story and worked selflessly to bring it to fruition, sharing his creativity, talent, and contacts in the literary world. Should you ever have the chance to work with Bill on a literary project, count yourself fortunate indeed. To Bill's multitalented colleagues that likewise became champions of this book, Elise Goyette, Kara Lack, and Patrick McDonald.

To Rob McQuilkin, my industrious literary agent who believed in this story from the get-go and coaxed it out of me, all the while cosseting me in wise counsel and encouragement; you are in every respect a gentleman in a world sorely lacking. I am singularly fortunate to be working with you, Lexi Wangler, and your talented Massie & McQuilkin team.

To Maxim Brown, my editor at Skyhorse Publishing, both a joy to work with and a sagacious guide; he made this book better at every touchpoint, as did copyeditor Alison Swety.

To my mother, June M. Wallace, and to the memory of my father, David S. Wallace, who believed that the world is a place of possibility, kindness, and wonder, and allowed me to travel to Ghana at the age of 16, when many of their friends surely thought they had taken leave of their senses. My parents believed without hesitation in their firstborn son—perhaps not so remarkable in and of itself, but they also believed in my dream—quite another thing altogether, and they did not once dissuade.

To my family, Linda E. Benfield, Hannah B. Wallace, Josh B. Wallace, and Benjamin B. Wallace, who indulged me for long years on this project and brought me joy at every step of the journey.

should be no colorings, no chemicals, no artificial ingredients of any kind.

Let the bar come to room temperature, then unwrap it. Observe the color of the chocolate. Milk chocolates tend toward lighter café au lait or caramel colors, and dark chocolates are, well, darker in color—deep, luxurious browns. Be wary of colors that simply don't look natural or appropriate. There shouldn't be a white powder or "bloom" on the surface of the chocolate. Bloom occurs when the cocoa liquor and cocoa butter separate, and the butter has risen to the surface of the bar. The physics of chocolate is such that the liquor and butter exhibit a sort of culinary entropy; over time they want to separate with the conspicuousness of oil and vinegar.

Now, using both hands, take the bar between the thumb and forefinger at opposite ends, and briskly snap the bar in half. Listen. Fine chocolate should give a satisfying snap. Study the fault line along the break: the chocolate face should be smooth. You don't want the chocolate to crumble. Neither should it be unduly soft.

Smell the chocolate. Inhale along the surface of the break. The aroma should be pleasing. It should smell like cocoa. If you try comparing several different chocolate bars at one sampling, you likely will notice quite a difference in aromas. What you don't want, though, is any sort of chemical or plastic smell—or a curious lack of aroma altogether.

Fine chocolate melts at body temperature. This indicates that the chocolatier hasn't skimped on cocoa butter, one of the most expensive ingredients in a chocolate bar. If you hold the chocolate in your hand for a minute or so, you should notice that it begins to melt. This body-temperature melting point is a key sign of quality. Some chocolate makers substitute a bit of vegetable oil or other types of fat to save money, and this will change the telltale melting point.

Now you are ready to taste the chocolate. Bite off a corner of the bar. Hold this morsel on your tongue for a moment before chewing, and gently press it against the roof of your mouth. You want the sharp corners of your chocolate fragment to begin to soften. Again, fine chocolate melts at body temperature, and the chocolate should begin to dissolve just slightly on your tongue.

Now chew it. Taste is entirely subjective; texture is not. You should not feel a waxy presence on the roof of your mouth, nor should the texture be especially granular. Smoothness is key. A creamy texture is another indication that the chocolatier hasn't skimped on cocoa butter.

Savor the chocolate. Do you sense a slight, subtle, fruity after-taste? Especially fresh, natural chocolate will result in an aftertaste that may hint of tart raspberries, say, or the piquancy of currants. Very fresh beans, not having been subjected to a six-week ocean voyage before processing as they transit from West Africa, for example, to Switzerland, naturally possess that fruity grace note. They contain no artificial flavors—because they do not need them.

Now you *know* . . .

OBRONI

AND THE CHOCOLATE FACTORY

Deɛ ɔkɔsee sɛ ɔtromoo brɛboɔ ɛdɛ no, wɔndi ngya no.
The one who told his mates the liver of the bush cow is a delicacy,
must partake in the feast.

"We must pay the forerunner the honor due to him."

CHAPTER 1

The Omanhene Idea

I have a chocolate company in Africa, near the foot of the Mampong Hills. I named it the Omanhene Cocoa Bean Company; *Omanhene* is the word in Twi, one of the major languages in Ghana, for "paramount chief" or "king." Our production facility squats forlornly in what's known as the Tema Heavy Industrial Area, in the artificially created port city of Tema, in Ghana, West Africa. The name alone tells you much about the history of the area. Tema was transformed during Ghana's ebullient, post-independence era of the late 1950s and early 1960s, when Five-Year Economic Plans heisted from the Soviet Union were all the fashion, and many senior Ghanaian ministers were treated to advanced degrees in Marxist-Leninist dialectics from Moscow University. Dredging a new deepwater port out of the shifting fluvio-deltaic sands of the Bight of Benin was not too ambitious a plan for a country brimming with optimism and postcolonial swagger.

That was a long time ago. Ghana was the Black Star of Africa, and heartily sick of kowtowing to Her Majesty. For savvy, charismatic Kwame Nkrumah—one of the Big Six, those dapper, London-educated gents who became the founders of modern Ghana—Pan-Africanism wasn't big enough. Nkrumah was a principal

3

advocate for the Non-Aligned Movement, that sprawling collection of postcolonial countries that found purpose and profit trafficking between the United States and the Soviet Union—like children of divorced parents, trying to curry favor and play the one off the other for financial and emotional well-being. I'm being only a bit cynical. Nkrumah famously said, "We look neither to the right nor to the left. We look forward." But he certainly enjoyed courting favors from both sides. Since Ghana's independence, the very word "Nkrumah" has commandeered a casual, imprecise ubiquity in modern speech. *Nkrumah this. Nkrumah that.* To this day, people still debate which current Ghanaian presidential candidate is the true Nkrumist (never "Nkrumah-ist" for some reason), as if we could ever know.

I am skeptical—and tired, frankly—of companies that claim to make the *best* chocolate or use the *best* cocoa beans, as if this were something that can be tested objectively or quantitatively. The word "best" rings hollow. Taste is subjective. Attributes of chocolate that connoisseurs adore may hold only passing regard to me. Still—and please indulge me here—it is fair to say that by many accounts, Ghana indeed grows some of the world's finest cocoa beans. They often fetch a premium over the benchmark Ivory Coast standard when traded on the international cocoa exchanges in London and New York. That's a quantitative measure of value. The venerable *Financial Times* some years ago touted Ghana as growing "the finest cocoa in the world," an endorsement by a respected, independent, honest broker. Not only does Ghana grow cocoa that is very good, it grows lots of it. Ghana has traded places, over the decades, with its Francophone sibling, Ivory Coast, as the largest exporter of cocoa beans on the planet.

Mention the word "cartel" and most people think of OPEC, the Organization of the Petroleum Exporting Countries, and the way it has, for most of its existence, skillfully manipulated the price of oil. Contrary to popular perceptions, OPEC includes countries as far removed from the Middle East as Ecuador; it comprises twelve countries that together control some 34 percent of the world's oil supply. Put another way, 66 percent of the world's petroleum lies *outside* of OPEC. The cartel does not control even half of the world's oil reserves.

Contrast petroleum with cocoa. Just two countries, Ghana and Ivory Coast, together account for a tad over 64 percent of the world's supply of cocoa. I've suggested, only half-jokingly, to the Ghana Cocoa Board (the national, quasi-ministry responsible for maximizing cocoa revenues and safeguarding the nation's cocoa industry) that the two countries should mend their postcolonial cocoa rivalry and behave more like a cartel, if they are serious about raising the wages of West African cocoa farmers. Happily, for chocolate consumers, no one at the Ghana Cocoa Board has taken my advice. As it is, Ghana (a former British colony) and Ivory Coast (Côte d'Ivoire, a former French colony) are locked in an annual competitive struggle to outdo each other for the crown of world's largest cocoa grower. This bilateral cocoa rivalry plays right into the hands of Big Cocoa, the three largest multinational cocoa processors: Roissy-Doucette, MacFinn, and V.S. Hope & Company. These corporations love nothing more than to see the two largest cocoa-growing countries engaged in a mad race to overproduce—an exercise that ultimately drives down the world price for raw cocoa beans, regardless of origin.

Truth be told, Ghana cocoa beans differ slightly from those exported from Ivory Coast. In most cases, a cocoa processor first needs to dry and clean Ivoirian cocoa beans, while beans from Ghana can go straight to roasting, since the Ghana Cocoa Board requires their top tier beans to be dried and cleaned *prior* to marketing them to customers.

But for decades, despite all this focus on *growing* cocoa in Ghana, there was almost no recognition of moving up the cocoa value chain and making confectionery from the nation's cocoa bean supply. Here was the paradox: Ghana, one of the two largest cocoa-growing countries in the world, produced no finished chocolate.

To be precise, when I started my company in 1991, Ghana produced *almost* no finished chocolate. The chocolate that had been attempted in Ghana was roundly acknowledged as some of the world's worst and had failed to sustain exports to any high-end consumer market. It was rumored to contain paraffin to keep it from melting in the Ghanaian heat. A pound of high-quality chocolate sells at a price many times that of a pound of raw cocoa beans, yet over the course of many decades, instead of producing quality chocolate, Ghana was content to sell its raw cocoa beans to processors and chocolatiers in Switzerland, Belgium, France, the Netherlands, and the United States.

Switzerland makes fine chocolate, of course, but how many cocoa trees grow in Zurich? In the vocabulary of the eighteenth-century economist David Ricardo, what *competitive advantage* does Switzerland enjoy, that Ghana could not more credibly assert? Comparative advantage in the realm of international trade is simply an admonition to *do what you do best, and trade for the rest.* It is a plea for companies and countries to identify those attributes that make them unique—and by "unique" Ricardo meant truly *one-of-a-kind,* if possible—and exploit those attributes in the marketplace. From an economist's point of view, there is no compelling *economic* reason, no underlying competitive advantage, why Hershey, Pennsylvania, is home to a large chocolate company. It is located very far from any cocoa farms, and it is an ocean away from the companies that historically have manufactured the machinery that converts raw cocoa into chocolate.

Consequently, my business began with a simple question: Why shouldn't Ghana make its own chocolate? I believed that Ghana should reap a bigger share of the downstream profits derived from its much-admired commodity. Though Ghana seemed content to sell beans for pennies a pound instead of making chocolate that sells for several dollars a pound, I believed strongly that Ghana could and should move up the cocoa value chain.

Ghana could truly make a fresher, more compelling chocolate by seizing its climatological and topographical advantage for growing cocoa. The country starts with an enviable, unassailable raw-material advantage over its Alpine competitors, whose climate is singularly inhospitable to the cultivation of cocoa trees. But an ascent of the cocoa value chain would require that Ghana procure both specialized production knowledge and machinery, both of which, happily enough, are available (at a price) and portable: you can hire experienced chocolatiers and fly them to Ghana, and you can likewise import German-built conches and roller mills. If you assemble *all* these components *in* Ghana, you could make chocolate with a unique value proposition—*freshness*—that should be competitive in the global market. And, according to economists, once you've achieved this result, then you ought to forgo other less-remunerative agricultural or manufacturing efforts and press your competitive advantage *hard*.

Thus the notion of comparative advantage in international trade, if taken literally, is both intellectually provocative and almost certainly politically untenable. Does it truly make sense to bet the farm on a single industry, no matter how lucrative? What about allocation of risk? Shouldn't a national economy bet on several industries, rather than just one? But to ignore the lesson of *uniqueness* in comparative advantage is to miss the opportunity to create long-term prosperity.

I raised this issue at a meeting of the World Economic Forum on Africa, in 2011. The panelists were discussing the importance of food security in each country—a topic that held an undeniably populist appeal. Who could possibly be against food security?

To achieve food security, some countries subsidized the growing of certain food crops that were not the sort of crops that could be easily or efficiently grown in their countries. The crops might require extensive irrigation, which upset best-practice land use, or they compelled a diversion of natural watersheds, causing other ancillary harms. Almost certainly, pursuit of such policy required a heavy government subsidy, one that would eventually prove economically unsustainable over time. So far as I could tell, "food security" seemed to be defined by most countries as "growing as much of your food domestically as you can, regardless of the cost or subsidy required." Such thinking struck me as a rebuke to the notion of global trade and its many benefits. At the question period, I made my way to the microphone.

"What if," I asked, "an African country made such wondrous chocolate that it captured significant foreign exchange revenues? Imagine that this country's chocolate sold abroad with great success, leading to a surplus account denominated in hard currencies—a surplus so formidable that the country could now afford to import rice and other foodstuffs instead of trying to grow them domestically? Isn't that a better, more economically sustainable result than trying to promote food security via artificial price supports?"

I'm transfixed by the idea of comparative advantage in all its implications. Switzerland, Germany, and Italy have excelled in cocoa-processing technology. They bend and polish stainless steel into the marvelous roller mills and ribbon blenders that coax cocoa beans into finished chocolate. They fabricate the jacketed kettles known as conches that gently warm the chalky cocoa mass over the course of many hours—days even—into luxurious molten chocolate. These Alpine countries are home to the companies that make the machines that make the chocolate. And hence, these countries also became adept at making chocolate itself. But these processing machines, once built, could be transported anywhere on the globe. Rarely, however, had they been purchased by companies willing to make chocolate in those tropical countries where cocoa is physically grown—where, I believe, the comparative (and thereby competitive) advantage resides. And when cocoa-processing machinery is placed in an origin country, the investors rarely try to craft finished chocolate designed for export markets. Why not, I wondered?

Somehow globalism as practiced during Africa's colonial scramble had devalued the natural advantages that should have been enjoyed by many African countries, rendering these countries mere repositories of raw materials awaiting exploitation by processors located throughout the globe. Africa had become the pantry for the world, a place where more enterprising nations abroad could stock their shelves with bauxite, gold, uranium, petroleum, rubber, diamonds, sugar, and cocoa.

"Globalism" shouldn't be a dirty word, I thought. Globalism once held promise. The algorithm was straightforward. Geographic competitive advantage (derived from the global scarcity of certain natural resources), when combined with education and technology, should hold some hope for creating enduring national wealth.

So I began my chocolate journey by thinking about globalization. Omanhene, though laughably smaller than many of our competitors, nonetheless competes in a global economy, and we have fashioned our company, very deliberately, to address head-on some of the most vexing issues surrounding globalization.

We recognize that the world is undergoing rapid globalization, but is globalization a good thing or bad? Just a generation or three ago, there was widespread agreement that nationalism, militarism, and expansionism led to the atrocities of World War II. To countries large and small, rich and poor, globalization appeared to be an antidote—perhaps the only antidote—to the abyss of war.

The Marshall Plan can be viewed as an unprecedented globalization effort to rebuild a broken and bankrupt Europe using US government funds, in the belief that economic prosperity and economic interdependence were the best ways to assure that war would be the choice of last resort when it came to solving international disputes. Think of the Marshall Plan as a global stimulus package, as deficit spending writ large for purposes of global economic recovery. Charged words perhaps in today's incendiary political environment, but in retrospect the Marshall Plan was worth every penny.

Today, however, globalization is shorthand for economic exploitation—a sort of "take it or leave it" economic determinism wherein a small country must accede to the demands of a large, multinational corporation. Why? Because that multinational might well have more economic value than the entire GDP of that small country, and consequently the small country acquiesces to the demands of the multinational, or else it won't have any foreign direct investment whatsoever. Walmart, after all, had gross revenues of some $486 billion in 2015, making it a far larger economic enterprise than the entire nation of Ghana, with its GDP of just about $32 billion in 2015. By this measure, Walmart is an economic engine over ten times the size of Ghana. Widespread frustration with the perceived exploitative influence of multinationals culminated in 1999, when massive public protests disrupted the World Trade Organization meeting in Seattle.

We had come full circle in the span of just fifty-four years, from 1945 to 1999. The word "globalization" changed meaning entirely—it changed from a positive force that underpinned the Marshall Plan to a menacing one that threatened jobs.

It is in this historical context that Omanhene was founded, as a multinational company that aspires to serve as a force of global good. All this goes for naught, however, if you don't produce a fairly-priced, delicious chocolate bar or a tin of hot cocoa drink mix that people will buy more than once. For me, economic viability over time is the very definition of sustainability.

So, I'd like to revisit my old friend David Ricardo and discern just what competitive advantage—other than exoticism and novelty—*I* might assert in the highly competitive global chocolate marketplace.

Crafting chocolate in a cocoa-growing country of origin provides a freshness advantage that legacy chocolate companies abroad simply cannot replicate. These European and American producers have to acquire raw cocoa beans, fumigate them, stuff them into the dark hold of a steamship, and subject the beans to a monthlong ocean voyage before processing them into chocolate. Our comparative advantage rests on freshness and authenticity.

The story of Omanhene is still very much a work in progress. I am not ashamed of this. I am not especially proud of it, either. It took more years than I care to admit before I stopped the incessant, daily worrying that nagged at me like a microeconomic harpy taunting me from my shoulder: "You will run out of money in two weeks! MacFinn will bury you! M&M Mars will copy everything you've done, and they'll do it better, faster, and cheaper! You think you can transform a nation's economy, do you? Such hubris!"

It took so many years to achieve positive cash flow that any venture capitalist would have bailed on the Omanhene project, executing their remorseless five- or seven-year "exit strategy," to use their sanitized nomenclature for quitting. So this is not going to be a book about the founding of the company per se. *That* book implies a sense of temporal certitude—a beginning, a middle, and an end—that does not seem truthful to the journey I've undertaken. That book would require me to rewrite history, and I won't do that. So this story covers the early years of what would become The Omanhene Cocoa Bean Company. It was a tumultuous, exasperating, and exhilarating period. It almost cost me my home, my wife (how perilously close it came to unraveling my marriage, I may never know), my sense of humor, my credibility (whatever that was worth), and, to quote Mr. Thomas Jefferson, my *sacred honor.* It was a helluva time. I wouldn't trade it for the world.

I didn't get into the chocolate business because I grew up eating a lot of chocolate. Nor did I start the company because I needed a capstone project for an MBA—indeed, I never went to business school. I went to law school, and for two years I practiced tax law in Washington, DC. I was miserable. But I soon left the firm, returned to my hometown of Milwaukee, and began working in the family wholesale T-shirt business, a low-margin enterprise in a brutally competitive market. Sensing that the company would soon face blistering competition from larger out-of-state competitors as a wave of consolidation racked the industry, I suggested we sell the business. I effectively told my father to put me out of a job. He took me up on my offer. I was twenty-nine years old.

And so, with time on my hands, I kept returning—the way you pull a favorite book off the shelf again and again—to memories of a remarkable summer, in a faraway country I hadn't seen in fourteen years.

Ɔhoɔ ani akɛseakɛ, nanso enhunu ɔman mu asɛm.
The big eyes of a stranger nevertheless do not permit them to see
everything in their new abode.

"The perception of the foreigner is never perfect."

CHAPTER 2

The Summer of 1978

The desert, some thirty-eight thousand feet below, seemed a casual, khaki joke. From this height, the Sahara was an expanse of undifferentiated sand dunes and hillocks, rock and wadi, as far as I could see. Holed up in the cabin of the jumbo jet, I felt the rise of claustrophobia—my personal shame. My heart raced, my stomach a cauldron of microwaved fondue and V8 juice. I popped up from my seat and scanned the fuselage looking for the emergency exit. Not that I'd actually do anything, but it helped to know I *could*.

My panic dissipated. Hours later, the jet heaved forward like a breaching whale, and we descended into Accra. As the plane gently rolled sideways, lining up its approach, I saw sections of the city spread out beneath us—streetlights, modest-sized buildings, and the headlamps of cars—points of light as random as raindrops. For so many hours, the high altitude exerted its aerodynamic sleight of hand; we seemed to hang motionless in the sky. Relative speed (or lack of it) masked the forward motion of the plane. Now, the wing lurched up and down, the displaced clouds confessing our speed as the plane accelerated earthward. Gilbert and Sullivan's *HMS*

Pinafore played on channel three. I couldn't help but hum along as I pictured the cast raising their arms in Britannic triumphalism: "He remains an Englishman! He remains an-Eh-eh-eh-eh-eh-eh-eh-eh-Englishman!"

The airport in Accra bore a passing resemblance to news clips I'd seen of Entebbe, my only frame of reference for African airports. The wan lighting, the low-set cement structures, paint worn thin by the equatorial heat, rusting fifty-five-gallon oil drums stacked near a terminal building set with jalousie windows, their glass louvers caked with dust. KOTOKA INTERNATIONAL AIRPORT was rendered along an exterior wall in large plastic letters, in a font so pedestrian that you couldn't help but wonder if anyone considered the value of using a more modern typeface simply to create an image of progress.

We nosed up to an Aeroflot jet, a tri-engine Tupolev, the Bolshevik Boeing. Détente on the tarmac. The door opened, and the oppressive heat hit me, even though the hour was late and the sun had set long ago. I'd never been to Ghana before, never felt anything like this anywhere. My response was astonishment, combined with a frisson of fear. *How will I breathe? Can I bear this heat?*

I paused at the top of the staircase and removed my powder-blue Camp Chippewa windbreaker, tying it about my waist, pulling the sleeves tight so the jacket wouldn't slip down. A Ghanaian woman with a clipboard reached for my crotch and violently tried to undo the knot, pulling off my jacket. "Ei, silly boy! What are you doing? Take that off."

I pulled back, shocked. Was she a thief? Why was she so angry? Why did a thief have a clipboard? A flashbulb popped. A journalist took my picture and asked for my name. What had I done?

Welcome to Ghana.

I made my way down the gangway, confused. Even the aircraft struggled to breathe in this heat, its engines sucking the tropical air, turbines spinning slowly down. The jet's chilled aluminum skin, frozen after six and a half hours at high altitude, drew moisture from the humid air and deposited it in small puddles around the fuselage. Every engine nacelle, fuselage rivet, wheel hub, and pitot tube was bejeweled in tiny droplets of water.

So this is what summer is like in equatorial Africa. Before leaving home, I'd done enough research to know that the climate in Ghana was different: low temperatures in Ghana were, on average, in the mid-70s—pretty much the summertime average high in Milwaukee. And I knew better than to expect jungle landscapes, like real-life Rousseau paintings, especially not in the city of Accra. But the riot of vegetation astonished me; greenery flourished, cascading over every wall, the scent of it perfumed the warm air around me. In the darkness, I could see the harsh fluorescent lights of Accra punctuating the cubist silhouettes of compact, leaden buildings that seemed to crouch close to the ground, even the ones that were several stories high. Milwaukee, with its proud Midwestern tradition of first-rate architecture preserved in many parts of town, seemed a far taller city. Yet there was a muscular energy here in Accra, one I couldn't define, and only part of it emanated from me. The whole airport seemed to vibrate and bustle, accompanied by loud voices in languages I didn't understand. It was thrilling—and I could tell I'd have trouble getting to sleep that night.

* * *

It was fitting that we landed on a Sunday. In Ghana, most people have a nickname that corresponds to the day of the week on which they were born, a tradition that three of the largest ethnic groups in Ghana—the Fanti, the Twi (Akan), and the Ewe—all follow:

17

Male Day Name	Day of Birth	Female Day Name
Kojo	Monday	Adwoa
Kwabena	Tuesday	Abena
Kwaku	Wednesday	Akua
Yaw	Thursday	Yaa
Kofi	Friday	Afua
Kwame	Saturday	Ama
Kwesi	Sunday	Akosua

Ghanaian "day names" lead to some confusion. Unlike a Russian novel, where a single character might have half a dozen different names (Pyotr, Pierre, Petroushka, the Count, Count Bezukhov, etc.), in Ghana, half a dozen people in your social circle might share the exact same name (Kofi, Ama, Kwame, Abena, Kojo, etc.). It's the difference between the illusion of a large population and the illusion of consanguinity—as if Russia needed to populate its vast geographic footprint artificially and Ghana preferred to keep things in the family.

Legend has it that the first white person ever to visit the area now known as Ghana arrived on a Sunday. Ever since, light-skinned people—often men and women alike—are called *kwesi obronis*, literally "Sunday foreigner" or colloquially "Sunday white man," often shortened to *Kwesi* or *obroni*. On the street, the appellation is said so fast and with such eagerness that it often sounds like "*Kwesi 'broni.*" There is no pejorative racial connotation at all. *Obroni* is almost always said with a welcoming smile and a wave. Starting the first morning in Accra, I heard cries of "*Ei, 'broni, 'broni!*" as soon as I set foot outside.

Are they trying to say hello to me?

But then I noticed that some of the Ghanaians I encountered were holding a newspaper and pointing to it. Thanks to the exquisite timing of that photographer, my picture was on the front page of the

Ghanaian Times, sent to record the arrival of three American high school exchange students. I didn't really understand why anybody would think this was newsworthy, but I decided to pick up a copy to send back to my parents, as proof that I'd made it this far safe and sound.

Over the next few days in Accra, all over town, Ghanaians I'd never seen kept greeting me: "*Ei, 'broni, 'broni!*" Had one newspaper photograph made me famous? You'd think I was a movie star.

You don't always get to choose your celebrity.

* * *

After a week in Accra, I was to spend most of my summer in Sunyani, the capital of Brong-Ahafo, one of ten administrative regions in Ghana. My first—but certainly not my last—encounter with a Ghanaian parastatal, or state-owned business, was riding the State Transport Corporation bus to Sunyani. The German-built Setra was packed full of smiling passengers for the 250-mile trip up-country from Accra. The happiness of the passengers no doubt stemmed from relief after queuing in line for over an hour to secure a seat. There were fold-down jump seats in the center aisle of every row, and I wound up on one of these, a claustrophobe's nightmare: an aisle full of seats meant there was no way to get to the door unless everyone in front of you exited first. The meandering ride took nearly ten hours. We stopped frequently to let off a bulbous market woman with her broad-brimmed hat, or to discharge a wiry youth who scuffled off the bus in red leather sandals. The bus driver sifted through the static of the radio until he found a brassy, high-life tune from the Super Uppers International or JK and the Boom Talents.

It was long past nightfall when, stiff-kneed and weary, I arrived in Sunyani. The bus lumbered into the lorry park, an unpaved patch of dirt off the main traffic circle. There was no depot, and apart from the bus's headlamps, no lights. I disembarked and squinted into the darkness. The air was a madrigal of scents: kerosene, fruit, and cigarettes. A man wearing a togalike robe motioned for me to hop in the back seat of a battered Toyota Corolla. For a moment, I thought he must be Yaw Brobbey, my host father. He was, instead, my host father's driver.

"You are most welcome," the driver said, bowing slightly and using the formal Ghanaian greeting.

"Thank you," I replied, thinking we had the conversation backward, since "thank you" usually precedes "you're welcome."

We rode silently along unpaved roads, the driver chewing a camphor stick as he hunched over the wheel, dexterously working the gearshift. Apprehensive and impatient, I tried to see anything in the darkness, but only the occasional cooking fire or lantern met my gaze. I knew that Sunyani wouldn't look like Milwaukee, but what *did* it look like? Was that a goat or a dog by the side of the road? I couldn't tell. At last the headlights fell on a heavyset, single-story concrete structure, and for the first time I saw my Ghanaian home, a rectangle of rooms surrounding an open courtyard. Yaw Brobbey waited to greet me with the kind of embrace that assured me immediately that he intended to take the role of "host father" seriously. He took me into the house and offered me two drinks: a glass of water and a bottle of Tata beer.

"This is customary, to welcome a guest," Yaw Brobbey explained, handing me the water.

"And the beer?" I asked.

Yaw Brobbey laughed. "This is, ah, *not* so customary!"

I started to drink the water, but he stopped me. "No, no, Steven. Like this." He spilled a few drops of water on the concrete floor, then drank. I followed his cue, as we poured libation to the gods, in honor of my arrival. The water was cold and tasted of clay as if it had been drawn straight from the earth. It's hard for a Milwaukee boy to admit, but at sixteen years of age, I didn't like the taste of beer, regardless of whether it was Schlitz or Pabst or Tata. *I do want to be polite,* I thought, *but*—and then, before I could resolve my dilemma, my twenty-one siblings entered the room to greet me with shy formality, one at a time. The younger children could barely conceal grins of excitement at their new *obroni* brother.

Yaw Brobbey showed me to my room; my brothers would be sleeping five to a bed so that I could have my own mattress. My father's room was right next door. He had three wives, one of whom was the widow of his deceased brother, now part of Yaw's family, by whom he had several children. Two wives slept in separate bedrooms at the far end of the house; though they passed my room to meet my host father, I was never once aware of any late-night rendezvous. The third wife lived at a midwife's house nearby, because she was heavily pregnant.

My first morning in Sunyani, I woke to what sounded like the laconic swish of brushes on a jazz drummer's snare. My sister Faustina was sweeping the patio with a passel of stiff reeds tied together at one end; the makeshift broom rhythmically scraped the cement. Roosters cawed in the fresh morning light. Yaw Brobbey greeted each day with a glass of scotch in one hand and a straight shaving razor in the other as he stood bare-chested in the courtyard. This space, I quickly learned, was central to almost everything the Brobbeys did. My sisters cooked succulent groundnut stew over an open fire in the courtyard. The boys chopped firewood here. Everyone washed their laundry here. The youngest played skipping games—like jump rope, but without the rope—that ended with the children clapping, hopping, and falling over one another with laughter. Here in the courtyard, too, Yaw (Dad) Brobbey dispensed an allowance to each of his children. Every few days, the children crowded around him as he pressed the worn cedi bank notes into their little palms.

The first morning, as every morning, Yaw stood shirtless, smiling, massaging his Santa Claus belly and extemporizing on all matters of life, love, and commerce. He tousled the hair of his sons and let his daughters try to wrap their arms around his midriff. Dad Brobbey gargled his scotch and sent a son to fetch more hot water from the charcoal fire. Then he grinned at me, raising his half-empty tumbler in a jovial toast.

"Steven, you would like?"

It was shortly after 7:00 am.

"Ah, Steven, it is *verrryyyy* fine. It will make you feel bettah."

Since my third day in Accra, I'd been fighting a terrible case of diarrhea. I shook my head and smiled, patting my stomach, smiling gamely.

"To your health then, Steven!"

The Brobbey house sat about ten yards back from the road, on the outskirts of Sunyani. Across the street, a small road curved into the distance, with a few homes scattered about, and chickens strutting as if they owned the place. Behind our house stood a fragment of forest, tall grass and fronded trees, their muscled trunks brocaded with vines. A cocoa-red dirt pathway snaked through the bush until it emerged in the yard of an elementary school. This was the shortcut to the town center and my host father's store, the Littlewood Grocery, a cramped kiosk in the center of Sunyani. The word "grocery" was foreign to most people in Ghana, I later learned, and confused some in town. The word represented Yaw Brobbey's aspiration to have a shop with global cachet; "grocery" conjured up visions of high street supermarkets with bright linoleum floors.

Sunyani seemed tidy, modest, and compact. Two-story concrete buildings lined dirt roads that converged at the city center. The *zongo*, the name for the often pitiable, heavily Muslim enclaves found in nearly every city in Ghana, lined one side of the road. Kwabena Kraa, the town goldsmith, had his forge there, and I often detoured so I could pass his shop as I walked to the Littlewood Grocery. I was transfixed by the boy who industriously pumped the bellows, as Kwabena annealed lumps of Obuasi gold. On the other side of the road was a wooden kiosk where the tailor pedaled an old Singer sewing machine, embroidering batik shirts with the traditional embellishment of whorls and spirals known as *jaromi*. The smell of Sunyani on my morning walk was redolent of warm earth. It was the scent of fried plantains, palm oil simmering in an iron cauldron, and decaying palm fronds.

Among all the citizens of Sunyani, Yaw Brobbey was one of the most prominent, and, like my own father, he was a remarkable teacher in the ways of business—his skill resting largely on his ability to listen earnestly to people and talk to them with credibility and a degree of modesty. He was chairman of the Brong-Ahafo United football club, a team that played in Ghana's premier league, which was unusual for such a small municipality. A high-spirited entrepreneur, Dad Brobbey held an import license, probably the only way a person *outside* the government could make serious money under the military dictatorship of General Ignatius Kutu Acheampong. An import license held the key to enjoying the good life in Ghana. Disco dancing at the Moustache Club or buying goat kebabs in the market—all this required money—and one could earn cedis with an import license. For those with a trader's mind and an entrepreneurial bent, an import license was better than the purest Obuasi gold.

My host father used his import license to buy a Ford tractor and three manual-transmission Toyotas. He leased the tractor to neighboring farmers and promoters working on small construction projects. They paid a high price to use the town's only working piece of heavy machinery. Dad Brobbey painted the fenders of two of his Toyotas orange, the Ghanaian livery for taxicabs. He had no trouble leasing the vehicles for a fee that included trading shifts as one of his personal drivers. Dad Brobbey liked to sit in the front seat next to his driver instead of the back, as if he could never comfortably delegate the task of driving and navigation. The third Toyota my father kept for himself.

He oversaw his little empire of diversified holdings from the back room of the Littlewood Grocery. Without the benefit of an MBA or classes on asset allocation and diversification of risk, Dad Brobbey crafted a portfolio of investments well-suited to the vicissitudes of Ghana's economy—an economy that, in 1978, was in ruinous shape. I had brought about $200 with me to last the summer. At one point, I briefly contemplated spending it all on a single bottle of Coca-Cola, when an evanescent spell of homesickness descended on me, but there was no supply of Coke—an imported beverage—to be found in all of Sunyani at *any* price. Ghana lived hand-to-mouth in 1978. On July 3, I wasn't surprised to hear that, in a sort of preemptive salute to the US Independence Day celebration, General Acheampong had been overthrown in a coup d'etat led by another soldier, General Fred Akuffo.

The novelty of seeing an *obroni*, and a relatively young one at that, in Brong-Ahafo in 1978, seemed a singularly pleasing and auspicious occurrence, like spying a leprechaun. Cheery cries of *"Ei! Kwesi 'broni!"* followed me everywhere. Sometimes the people knew who I was—"Brobbey's American!"—and sometimes they didn't. It didn't seem to make any difference. *"Kwesi 'broni!"*

On quiet days, I often wandered to the store through the yard of the elementary school behind our house. If I was lucky, the children would be out for recess, for I was a celebrity. A schoolboy might spot me when his soccer ball rolled astray, and he would approach, smiling gregariously and shaking my hand, pumping my arm furiously.

"Good morning, sir!"

"Good morning! I am not a sir."

"You are very welcome! Are you well today, sir? Are you very well this morning?"

Soon his teammates would swarm me, and then, overcoming their shyness, dozens of schoolgirls joined us. So many schoolchildren, all inquiring after my health, wishing me a good morning, and hopping up and down with excitement as they practiced, perhaps for the first time, their textbook English on a real *obroni*. One girl grabbed my forearm. My tan skin flushed white at the spot where she poked me. Her mates found this blushing fascinating. In an instant, everyone wanted a turn, dozens of school children poking me with unrestrained glee, intently regarding my skin blush as they pressed their sturdy little digits into my sunburned skin, all the while chirping *"Obroni, obroni!" The best recess of the entire year.* I was spared further experimentation by a school bell, rung by a worried teacher who stood, shaking the bell for all he was worth, on the porch of the school.

When I arrived at the Littlewood Grocery, I would sit and listen to the men who congregated around the counter, chatting in Twi. I barely understood what they said. If it weren't for the demonstrative facial expressions and the dramatic intonations of the men, I could not have followed the conversations *at-TALL* (the quintessentially Ghanaian pronunciation, as if the two words were one, with the accent on the second syllable, pronounced similar to the word "atoll").

"Ei! Kwesi 'broni, wo ho te seyn?" "How are you?"

"Me ho-yɛ," I answered. "I am fine."

This would result in much laughter, chattering in Twi, and enthusiastic handshakes, followed by the Ghanaian finger snap: you shake hands, and then, as you release, you keep your middle finger extended and simultaneously snap your middle finger to your thumb as your partner's middle finger slides away.

Then I added for comic effect, *"Me ho-yɛ, pah, pah, pah!"* "I am very, very, *too* much fine!"

"Whoa, Steven, you are *toooo* funny, ei!" a man the size of a middle linebacker said as he adjusted his traditional robe over his shoulder, shaking his head in wonder. Mr. Kwame Adjei-Frimpong, a friend of Yaw Brobbey's, constantly battled the force of gravity that kept pulling his robe down off his shoulder. Adjei-Frimpong's cloth often drooped about his belly like a sagging diaper, revealing pendulous breasts that jostled like bowls of *fufu* when he laughed.

We carried on like this for quite a while; I could spend most of the morning imitating their Twi as they laughed at my antics.

The Littlewood Grocery consisted of a counter, behind which were rows of shelves, like those in an old-time general store. Yaw Brobbey artfully arranged boxes of nails, tins of tea, jerry cans of kerosene, and bottles of schnapps along the shelves to give the impression that business was far brisker than it really was. In truth, there were only a few times all summer when anyone came into the store to buy something—and each time it happened, Yaw Brobbey treated the event more as an interruption of a good conversation than as the raison d'être of the establishment. A customer would enter, scan the shelves, more in hope than in anticipation; the moribund economy had a depressing effect on both mood and pocketbook. Then, the customer would look expectantly at the men, who regarded any interloper with polite indifference. An uncomfortable silence. The customer would sigh, turn, and leave, the departure barely disrupting the political discussion taking place.

In Ghana, then as now, the worse the government, the more people talk about it. It is a shame, I tell myself, that people don't talk so much about politics when a government gets things right, delivers basic services. The reward of good governance—government with a light, unobtrusive touch—is that everybody simply goes about their business unaware.

Only once did my host father invite me into the small back room where he had his private office. A young assistant came out to the front, deferentially interrupted the political discourse going full throttle, and motioned for me to follow him. He led me into a windowless closet of a room so small that the desk, behind which my host father sat, nearly filled the room. Yaw Brobbey must have climbed over this desk to get to his chair, no small feat for a man of his girth.

"Steven, are you well?" He was inquiring after my health, not just extending a polite greeting; my amoebic dysentery was fast becoming something of a local legend. "Shall I cash traveler's checks for you? Four times the bank rate?"

His cherubic eyes smiling, he penciled the exchange rate in the margin of a green baize ledger, the kind with leather trim on the corners. A small wax candle was the only source of light in the room.

"Whatever you think is best."

Dad Brobbey nodded his approval and resumed his calculations as I stood waiting. I expected he might ask about my day, or else pay me right then and there. Perhaps he would offer me a scotch. He did nothing. His assistant tapped me on the shoulder, as if furiously pecking out a disaster message on an old-fashioned telegraph key, and ushered me out of the room without a word.

The longer I observed Yaw Brobbey in his general store, the easier it became to discern the shifts in his character. Focused and serious when he dealt with money, my host father transformed into a jovial elf when socializing. And yet the socializing itself was integral to conducting business. Socializing comprised sharing information, striking deals. Unwittingly, I began my education in how to do business in Ghana.

Some days, Dad Brobbey took me to meet some friends at a nearby Social Security and National Insurance Trust (SSNIT) rest house, a small establishment owned, as was almost everything at this time, by the government. "Government" in this context could mean the national government in Accra, or the Brong-Ahafo regional government, or some outpost of a ministry, say Road and Transport, or a quasi-government entity like the SSNIT, Ghana's state pension fund.

Dad ordered Gulder beers for us all and introduced me to his friends. The beers arrived glistening with condensation, and while the men chattered away, I stacked the bottle caps on the worn Formica tabletop. My host father talked about football, how BA United would fare against Accra Hearts of Oak or Sekondi Hasaacas, before he turned to the price of cocoa, yams, or fuel, which he pronounced *foo-el.* From time to time, he smiled at me and made an effort to include me in the conversation, conducted almost entirely in Twi.

"Ei! Me kaa sɛ ma hyɛ bɔ sɛ mennware de dii agorɔ Kɛkɛ."

"Paaaa!"

"Yo, tsk, tsk." One of the men shook his head in disgust, affirming the mood of the others at the table. Was he Kwame? Kofi? Kojo? What with the beer, the mind-numbing humidity, and the conflating of names that begin with the letter "K," I struggled to keep it all straight.

"Ah, yes, Steven," Yaw Brobbey began. All eyes turned expectantly toward me. I nodded. "You know the meaning of *kwesi 'broni*?" Dad Brobbey asked. This was the setup for what was becoming the longest-running comedic performance in Brong-Ahafo—a sort of doppelgänger minstrel show where I performed in whiteface.

I smiled and nodded with a look that said, "Do I ever!"

The other men thought this was hilarious and perhaps even highly unusual—though I was bombarded with *kwesi 'broni* in every public space, including twice by the waitstaff as I sat *right here at this very table.* You'd have to be an idiot not to pick up what *kwesi 'broni* means within the first fifteen minutes of arrival in Ghana.

"Ei, 'broni, 'broni! You are too clever-o," one of the men hooted.

I was vain enough, and desperate enough for attention, to take this as a compliment. The conversation quickly reverted to Twi and continued without me. Yaw Brobbey was in his element. Talking business and football, expounding on politics with friends, drinking cold beer, and showing off his newest son, his *obroni* son, child number 22. Soon to be number 23. My forearms were pleasantly wet from the puddle of cold beer on the table, a sort of makeshift alcoholic air conditioning. Slouching down in the lawn chair, I wallowed in the recklessness of the evening. I caught the word "cedi" as the conversation veered unexpectedly into English. The friend laughed and bent forward in mirth.

"Like 'Bugs,' yes?"

"Oh yes, Bugs Bunny!" Dad Brobbey answered. "Twenty-thousand cedis for a rabbit farm. Bettah than chickens-o. I should like that *very* much indeed!"

"Ei, I tried to get a loan from the Agric bank to plant yams and *yo* . . ." The friend's voice trailed off sadly before he said, "They want 43 percent interest on the loan." He sighed, nodding dejectedly. "Forty-three percent! That is *too* hard. I tell the banker, 'Ei! Forty-three percent? How can I pay you back? I should plant diamonds, not yams!'"

Afterward, Dad Brobbey helped me into the back seat of the Toyota. The plastic seats were still warm from the late-afternoon sun, and they cracked softly as I settled in. The sky was dark. Too many stars for one sky. I pulled my knees to my chin, a now-familiar posture that helped relieve the dysentery stomach cramps. I turned my head so I could better see the azure glow of the dashboard. Dad Brobbey lit up one of his Dunhill cigarettes—one of the few imported items that found its way into the local market—and I dozed off to the soft crush of bald tires on the dirt road.

Some days, Dad Brobbey took me to Techiman, about forty miles from Sunyani. I looked forward to these business trips, trips that got me out of the house, with its exasperating lack of privacy. I wondered whether my host siblings resented my time with their father. I did the math. If he were to devote just five minutes alone with every child and with each wife just once a day, it would consume a full two hours. I got several hours a day with Yaw Brobbey, and that must have had consequences for the family and my role in it. But I could not discern even a whiff of jealousy; the family's domestic dynamic comprised complacency, resignation, and a sort of gender-specific inevitability, with the girls tending the fire and cooking, and the boys lolling about, gathering wood, and finding ways to pass the long afternoons, waiting for the next meal.

Techiman was a typical town in the Brong-Ahafo region of Ghana. The ever-present, cocoa-colored dirt imparted a foppishly pink hue to many of the mud-brick or concrete houses, paint faded, dusty. Dad and I walked around the market, and he bought me a kebab of goat meat, crisp with pepper and ginger, one of my very favorite Ghanaian treats. The butcher, working behind his brazier, wielded a broad cleaver, hacking a dark slab of meat, effervescent with flies that alit as the blade hit home. A boy, presumably his son, coated the cubes of raw goat in a dry rub of spices by rolling the meat in a calabash.

By late morning, I began to feel the familiar queasiness in my stomach. I was anxious now to return home. We started back in the car, only to stop at what seemed like damn near every village on the road between Techiman and Sunyani. Dad had friends everywhere. He expounded enthusiastically on business matters with animated hand gestures; he was the Toscanini of the tabletop, pausing only to take a swig from his Tata beer or to declaim, sotto voce, a furtive recitative on Ghanaian politics. Dad Brobbey's dynamic range was impressive. So was my gastrointestinal distress. I repaired to the back seat of the Toyota, doubled over with cramps.

Yaw Brobbey found me there. I tried to compose myself, but he saw that I was in agony. He crossed himself. "Steven, you are unwell?" he asked.

"I'll be all right," I said, half-tempted to cross myself, too.

I wondered how Dad Brobbey's three wives squared with pontifical doctrine, but I already knew the answer: it didn't matter. This is Ghana. To an outsider, it might seem that rules were bent, ignored, or enforced with no sense of outward consistency—*but*, once you'd been here awhile and gotten culturally attuned a bit, you saw that the approach to rules bore an internal calibration that makes perfect sense. Besides, Yaw Brobbey was a generous man, both with his money and his amorous affections; so as far as I was concerned, the world needed more people like him.

* * *

One day at the Littlewood Grocery, I didn't feel like sitting quietly, respectfully, while Dad Brobbey and his friends talked politics. Interrupting them, I spoke up: "We've sent a man to the moon."

"Ei! *Kwesi*, you are *too* funny-o."

"Several times," I asserted.

"Why do you say these things, Steven?"

Adjei-Frimpong, sucking on a betel nut, translated my claims into Twi for the amusement of his two compatriots, who were passing another somnolent morning at the Littlewood Grocery. It struck me that the name of the store bore a comic, sexual irony, given my father's philoprogenitive accomplishments. "Littlewood" indeed.

"I am serious, Steven. Ei! Why do you say these things?" Adjei-Frimpong looked hurt, gesturing palms up.

How to answer his question? If I'm honest, I should admit I started making these indecorous claims about the United States' astronautical superiority to shift attention back to me. (Far from my most mature act, I admit, and I am ashamed to this day for my behavior.) But on this particular day, having battled dysentery for several weeks, I was exhausted. And I was upset, frustrated that my capacity to communicate in Twi was good enough only to give me the communication skills of a two-year-old. I could no longer keep up appearances. I was . . . tired. Tired of the unrelenting heat, tired of the singsong cadence of Twi. Tired of sitting for hours in polite silence, waiting for my comic pantomime turn—*The Kwesi Obroni Show.* Tired of the aggressive fluorescent fixtures that harshly lit every home, kiosk, and rest house in the entire country. Tired of the spavined, broken-winded Binatone air conditioners whose unrelenting drone makes human speech such a chore that every conversation becomes an exhausting echolalia of "I beg of you, can you repeat that?" Tired of amoebic dysentery. Tired of television sets turned full volume to compete with those crappy, plastic oscillating fans, dashing any hope of holding a coherent conversation. And don't get me started on what was being shown *on* television. *Most of all, I'm sick and tired of being sick and tired.*

But I kept all of this to myself, and when Adjei-Frimpong asked, "Why do you say these things?" I replied simply, "Because it's true."

"*Kwesi*, how do you do all this?"

"We launch men into space using huge rockets—rockets much taller than anything I see here." I scoured the landscape, my eyes finally resting on some palm trees lolling in the heat, their narrow trunks framing a radio transmitter far in the distance.

Adjei-Frimpong regarded his companions with wonder. Had he been making fun of *me*? Did he, perhaps, understand liquid oxygen propulsion and telemetry far better than I, but was he questioning me for *his own amusement*? Who was rising to whose bait?

"I am sorry, Steven," he smiled modestly, "what you speak of is magic." Adjei-Frimpong gestured toward me and asked, "*Kwesi*, here, would like a cola nut?" as one miraculously appeared from within the folds of his robe.

* * *

In the early part of the summer of 1978, Ghana's military dictatorship was on friendly enough terms with the Ivory Coast that the two countries planned a paved, multilane interstate motorway, crossing the border at a designated, mutually agreeable site. The Ghanaians told apocryphal stories of motorways in Africa that stopped abruptly at a border, one country unwilling to link its road at a site selected by their neighbor. They were stuck with two roads that did not connect at all, laying waste to the entire transnational enterprise.

The Ghanaian-Ivoirian road, however, was to be a real Western-style motorway with comfortably wide shoulders and gleaming rest stops. Visions of a first-class autobahn lit up the imagination. It would demonstrate that two African countries could, at long last, work together on a public works project. It would show they could surmount their realpolitik trade policies—small-minded, protectionist policies curiously at odds with the grand Pan-African socialist theories that underpinned nearly all the continent's independence movements. Finally, a step *forward*! And it would come through Sunyani.

That was the plan, anyway.

As luck would have it, Dad Brobbey's friend Mr. Danso-Manu owned a suitable piece of property on the outskirts of Sunyani, adjacent to where the new motorway was supposed to be built. The enterprising Ghanaian intended to cash in on the new highway, and he was constructing a seven-story hotel.

"Yes, I shall be very happy when the highway is finished," Mr. Danso-Manu said, arms akimbo as he surveyed the outlying savannah. The construction site lay at the end of a makeshift utility road surrounded by brilliant bottle-green vegetation. I didn't see any sign of the highway.

"When will the road be finished?" I asked, wondering silently, *When will the road be started?* The bucolic landscape gave no hint of road construction, not even a lone surveyor's flag.

"Ei! Things are very bad here, now, Steven. Ahaaaa . . ." His voice trailed off in a particularly Ghanaian exhalation—part sigh, part ellipses—that invites commiseration. "Everything is being rationed." Mr. Danso-Manu stood scowling at the rough-hewn, gray lattice of concrete pillars that might someday be his hotel. "You cannot get concrete *at-TALL*! Come, I will show you my hotel. Would you like a beer?"

"No, thank you." It was not yet ten o'clock in the morning, and my digestive difficulties hadn't improved.

"I will drink, myself, then, if you don't mind."

"Please, go right ahead. I'm not feeling too well." I grimaced, patted my stomach, and debated whether to try and add my own "Ahaaa." Maybe that way, he'd understand how I felt; maybe he'd even feel sorry for me. But it wasn't an easy decision. Ever since my first hours in Ghana, I'd been trying to mimic the cadence, inflection, and timbre of Ghanaian English, in the hope it might help me culturally fit in. *Ei! Too soon to tell how this might play in public. It might not work at-TALL, and I would only embarrass myself and my host family-o.*

Mr. Danso-Manu seemed perturbed that I didn't wish to join him in a drink. No doubt I had committed another social faux pas. To my young eyes, Ghanaians lived by a bewildering set of social conventions. Every day, I stumbled over such simple social graces as how to shake hands with several strangers (start on the right—*but my right or theirs?*) and the way the Ghanaians poured out a bit of a libation before drinking any of it, whether it was a glass of water or a tumbler of scotch. The trick was to pour a few precious drops, not spill your beverage and make an unseemly puddle, but it was yet another trick I hadn't mastered.

"Here will be the disco." Mr. Danso-Manu stretched out an arm like a vaudeville emcee introducing the next act. He gestured to a section of floor checkered in black-and-white linoleum. It was the only finished floor in the building. The rest of the ground floor was simply poured concrete. A pile of rebar rusted in a corner.

"You can see how bad the economy is. Look, no walls." Indeed. The entire building was open to the elements. Only concrete columns and poured floors had been completed. There weren't any fixtures, save for two gleaming toilets that reposed off to one side.

"Ah, yes! Here will be the facilities. One for the gents and one for the ladies."

Two toilets. For a seven-story hotel. *Well, it's a start.*

I saw no workers anywhere, and I asked Mr. Danso-Manu if he was overseeing construction himself.

"Oh yes, Steven. I am making sure things proceed smoothly. I studied in the UK, you know. Three degrees." He set his beer down on the toilet seat and, with studied deliberation, presented his business card as if he were a barrister revealing the key exhibit to the jury:

K. DANSO-MANU

M.A., LL.B. (CANTAB), B.L. (GRAYS INN)

I never doubted his degrees. I put his card in my wallet.

He pointed out what one might, with considerable imagination, suppose to be an elevator shaft. It was empty. "I am trying to get a lift," he explained, "but they are very costly."

No doubt his lift would be installed and his hotel would be completed long before the laborers started clearing a path for the new motorway. "Is there any chance that the plan will change?" I asked. "What happens if the government decides to move the road to the other side of town?"

Too late, I realized that I had just raised a delicate subject, one that Mr. Danso-Manu probably didn't want to think about, much less discuss with a teenager.

"I do not think that would be wise," he said calmly. "The road will be built here. I have a cousin with the ministry in Accra. No, the road will pass right by here." He meticulously pointed out the projected route, his elegant finger tracing a line in the air.

What ministry? I wondered. Even this American schoolboy knew that Ghana was burdened with nearly two dozen ministries, including the Ministry of Roads and Highways and the Ministry of Transport—either of which would, at first blush, seem to bear responsibility for a motorway project. Who was in charge? Plus, there were the ministries of Trade and Industry, and Foreign Affairs and Regional Integration, both of which could either promote or frustrate the planned highway to the Ivory Coast.

I hoped Mr. Danso-Manu's cousin was well placed. I wondered if he was really a cousin. In Ghana, it's common to refer to a close friend or business colleague as "my cousin," if they are your age contemporary; "my uncle or aunt," if they are your senior; and "my brother," if they are particularly close and especially when there is a favor to be begged—even though in each case, there is no actual consanguinity. *"My cousin, I beg of you, please understand that I cannot pay back the money this week." "Ei! My wife is too cross with me. Can I stay with you, tonight, my brother?"*

Mr. Danso-Manu and I stood in silence, and I found myself beginning to share his optimism. Despite the rationing of concrete, intermittent water, and unreliable electricity, Mr. Danso-Manu wrested enough material from God-knows-where to build a seven-story hotel frame in the middle of a cassava field on the far side of Sunyani. Two toilets, a disco dance floor, and space for an elevator—quite an achievement, even for a man with three degrees. If he could pull off this much, why shouldn't he succeed?

* * *

By my fourth week in Sunyani, it became unavoidably clear that I was not going to get over my dysentery on my own. If wishful thinking were a cure, I'd have felt better the second or third day. And I couldn't bear the sense that I was disappointing Yaw Brobbey, that my illness was a form of weakness that somehow reflected on him. He never said as much, at least not out loud, but I saw it in his eyes.

Matters weren't helped by the fact that I'd been eating so much *fufu*. *Fufu* is an Akan staple, a gelatinous starch made from pounding together boiled plantains and cassava, served in a calabash and covered with the most delectable goat or fish stews. You don't chew *fufu* so much as you swallow it whole, without chewing at all. The Brobbeys ate *fufu* at almost every meal. What was I supposed to do? Ask the family to cook something else, just for me, when the rest of them—two dozen people—were perfectly content to eat this starch-heavy staple? If I were an exchange student in Ireland (or Wisconsin, for that matter), would I ask my host family to stop serving me

36

potatoes? But I couldn't help it. In my current state, there was no way I could digest *fufu*, day in and day out.

At last I said to Yaw Brobbey, "Can I see a doctor soon?"

"Yes, Steven. We will go inside and see a specialist, Dr. Sarwar."

A specialist? In diarrhea?

The clinic in Sunyani reminded me of an old railroad depot. Long, wooden benches filled the main waiting hall. On each end of the waiting room were examination rooms. One small boy clutched a rubber sandal in his hand, his dark eyes following my every *obroni* move. The enameled blades of a slowly turning ceiling fan sifted together the sounds of whining children, the percussive maternal rebukes, the wailing babies, and the braying infirm. I took stock of all this and immediately felt better. Comparatively, I had little to complain of.

"Steven, here is Dr. Sarwar."

"Hello, Dr. Sarwar," I said with a meek smile, my stomach beginning to cramp for the umpteenth time. I started conducting my minute-quick toilet triangulation, a calculation of just how far the nearest lavatory might be and what obstacles might prevent quick access. An obese man blocking an aisle? A small child awkwardly using crutches like huge articulated locust legs to negotiate his way? An elderly woman incapacitated by some physical handicap? All would require an alternate route.

"Dr. *Sar*-war," said the meticulous Punjabi, coaching me.

"*Sar*-war," I dutifully repeated.

"No, say, '*Sar*-war.'"

"*Sar*-war," I intoned; the good doctor looked at me as if I were linguistically a lost cause.

"*Sar*-war. Okay. You are not well? That is too bad. I was the same when I first came to Ghana years ago. From Chandigarh. Ah! The food here is so very spicy—more than India!"

What possible circumstances persuaded Dr. Sarwar to leave India to come to Sunyani, of all places? Both countries teemed with their share of sick people, according to the American popular imagination. Could my doctor with the Nehru-collared lab coat have been defrocked from practicing medicine on the subcontinent? What type of transgression would merit such a punishment?

"Steven, I want you to drink this." He handed me a glass of white liquid that looked as if sticks of schoolroom chalk had been grated into water. The liquid smelled clean, it smelled . . . *cold*. I looked at Yaw Brobbey, who had gone to such trouble on my behalf, his invalid *obroni* son who couldn't stomach the most common of local foods. Yaw Brobbey nodded kindly and raised an empty hand in an imaginary toast to my health. I took a small sip, barely enough to swallow. I just couldn't manage to choke down the astringent, metallic-tasting liquid.

"Please, you must try. It will stopper you up," the doctor said encouragingly.

"It's hard to get down," I said. "Do you have anything else to drink?" I was the most ungrateful patient imaginable.

"You can wash it down with a mineral when we get home," Yaw Brobbey said. A "mineral" was a carbonated soda, such as the locally bottled Orange Fanta, a rare treat. The doctor looked dismayed, unused to such a recalcitrant patient, and his tight lips pursed even thinner. His body language looked as if he were about to say, "Why do these American *obronis* come to Ghana anyway?"—but he relented and allowed me to take the glass home with me.

"You must also have a jab, Steven," Dr. Sarwar added. "Your father will show you where to go. You will please give them this." Dr. Sarwar handed me a slip of paper.

"Thank you, Dr. *Sar*-war."

"Please remember to drink this medicine," he said, with a look of forlorn kindness. A softening. "I remember how it was when I first came to Ghana. Oooooh! I felt weak for six months!"

I could tell that poor Yaw Brobbey, used to being in control of people and situations, invincible in his Toyota and sandals, felt personally responsible for my ill health. In an awkward gesture, he put his arm around me. I leaned into his warm girth. Yet this made me feel even more strongly like a complete embarrassment to him and to myself. I fought back tears.

"We will make you *bettah*, Steven," he said gently. And then he beamed. "Our food is quite hot, quite spicy indeed!"

I was thankful that I didn't have to choke down the vile-tasting medicine in front of Yaw Brobbey and Dr. Sarwar. Weeks of eating *fufu* had given me a hypersensitive gag reflex. By now, I was unable to swallow anything at all without a strong urge to retch. I preferred to drink the chalky potion in the privacy of my room, where I could gag in solitude. By comparison, the prospect of getting an injection didn't seem so bad. I waited in line for my turn behind a white-linen modesty screen. Maybe it was the tiny sip of chalk water, but for a moment I began to feel better.

"Please, sir. Step over here," said the nurse. Like so many Ghanaians, she looked preternaturally young, and her gorgeous skin no doubt belied her true age by two decades or more. Her serious mien, the result of attending to an unrelenting succession of sick Sunyani faces, suddenly brightened at the prospect of injecting an *obroni*.

"Come here," she said, motioning to me. An assistant took my slip of paper and chose a vial of medicine from a table strewn with cotton balls and tiny glass bottles. In a shallow enameled pan, four thick needles soaked in antiseptic solution the color of Jamaican rum. "Drop your pants, please. And bend over."

The modesty curtain was imperfectly placed—perhaps intentionally? As I bent forward, I can see that most of the waiting room stared at my pale buttocks. The chatter grew quiet. Curious dark faces regard the impending spectacle with a combination of polite fascination and glee. The assistant fished out one of the needles submerged in the pan and screwed it atop the hypodermic. "Bend over tighter, sir."

A low groan escaped from me as the needle pushed deep into my buttocks.

Sometimes you have to feel worse in order to feel better. But there was comfort in the expectation that my remaining days in Sunyani wouldn't be defined by toilet triangulations and cramps and endless embarrassment. By morning, I felt slightly, perceptibly better.

* * *

On my last night in Sunyani, I emerged from my bedroom after spending three hours packing my bags. I couldn't explain why the task was so challenging. It's not as if I accumulated a lot more stuff than I had when I came here. *Maybe I don't really want to leave*, I thought.

And yet I did! I missed familiar food and could barely remember what it was like not being sick. I was ready for my own bed and my real brother and my real parents and a thousand other comforts of home. *And yet—*

Yaw Brobbey was waiting for me. He held out a Tata beer.

"To you, Steven."

"To you, Dad."

"I have lived all my life in this district. I have never traveled too far abroad," he said thoughtfully. "Someday, maybe I will come to America, and you can teach me."

"I'd like that," I said.

"A man on the moon!" He snorted, shaking his head. "Well, many things are different in America. But maybe *you*, you will be a little more Ghana now. You know, I did not think so, not when you came here."

"I didn't think so, either," I admitted. "I'm still not sure I'm very Ghana. Not *at-TALL*."

Dad Brobbey laughed. "Oh, yes, you are a little more Ghana now."

"Definitely more Sunyani than anybody else at my school."

He laughed again. "You are a good son, Steven. I have many sons, you know—but only one *obroni*."

The beer still tasted terrible. But sweeter, somehow.

"Now come, Steven. You must have your dinner. Goat stew!" Then he added, with a sly smile, "And *fufu*."

* * *

In some ways, I was aware already that Yaw Brobbey was right, and that my journey had led me to some small purchase of understanding about Ghana. Back in Accra, on the day of my departure for Milwaukee, I watched fresh-faced college students and earnest missionary groups arriving at the airport; many, I surmised, were making their first visit to this remarkable country. I wondered what sort of conclusions *they* would draw in three months' time.

Not all my thoughts were so cerebral; there were more startling aperçus. These new arrivals seemed impossibly *white*, for one thing. I was no longer so used to seeing Caucasians—and I didn't have the chance to look at myself often in a mirror in Sunyani. Now that I was back in Accra, I found it odd to regard my own visage. (Where was *my* color?!) In the airport, a group of ardent, young American evangelicals huddled in prayer with Father Bob, his guitar case next to a backpack. No doubt, they came to Accra to spread the word of God. Did they realize that Ghanaians are among the most devout evangelical Christians in the world? And what of the earnest Ivy Leaguers who came bringing campus feminism to this firmly matriarchal society—did they have any idea that women were part and parcel of the leadership of this country and culture—and had been quietly running families, companies, civic institutions, and ministries for decades?

A Pan Am 707 idled on the tarmac—*is there not a more perfect embodiment of American exceptionalism?* As I entered the cabin, I paused just before stepping over the aluminum threshold. I wondered if I'd ever see Ghana again. I had no reason to believe that I would.

*Wo bas a asa bɔne a, se no sɛ: w'asa yi ɛnyɛ fɛ; na ɛnse no
sɛ: ɔra tete wo ho gu mu.*
If your child dances clumsily in public, be bold in saying it;
do not placate him.

*"If your child performs poorly, admonish him;
do not say, 'you are doing a good job.'"*

CHAPTER 3

Dancing Clumsily

Ten years later, daydreams of Sunyani still preoccupied me, even back in Milwaukee, where I worked for the family T-shirt business, which my father affectionately and modestly referred to as "the rag trade," or the "the *schmatta* business." Instead of admonishing me to continue in the practice of law in Washington, DC, Dad welcomed me home enthusiastically. With me on board, the family business would extend for a third generation—or so we thought. I took a 60 percent pay cut to work with my father. I thought it a fair deal.

I called my father "DW"—his initials—as did everyone at the office, no matter how junior. The practice was started by my younger brother Jonathan when he was twelve or thirteen, and it surprised schoolmates when we'd call our father by his initials. "Does it bother you that we don't call you Dad?" I asked him once.

DW laughed. "I'm just happy we all still speak to each other so often," he said. "And with love and affection. Who cares what you call me?" Titles meant little to him. People meant everything.

Working alongside DW, I quickly realized that I was nearly as ignorant of his business practices as I'd been of Yaw Brobbey's. Granted, I'd grown up with the family business all around me, wearing sample shirts and sweaters for as long as I could remember, seeing my mother and father modeling in the company catalog. But I had a lot to learn.

DW loved coming to the office, reveled in working with his staff, and derived satisfaction from keeping inventory in place and a column of numbers balanced to the penny. From an old building in Milwaukee's Third Ward, the former garment and produce district, Midstates Sportswear sold blank T-shirts and sweatshirts to the embroidery and screen-printing trade. We were wholesale distributors, buying big boxes of T-shirts, breaking bulk, and selling shirts by the dozen or even by the piece. Between all the sizes, colors, and styles we maintained in inventory, the number of "SKUs," or stock-keeping units, topped three thousand. My father plotted all his purchasing by hand, without the benefit of a computer. His favorite use of data-processing technology was taking dozens of sheets of the now obsolete, green-and-white striped, fan-folded, tractor-fed computer paper, and laying them out on the conference table as scratch paper. DW liked a large canvas. Then, using a pencil and a few pink rubber erasers, he'd decide how many youth-size medium, navy blue, all-cotton, ringer T-shirts we needed for the coming year. And he got it right with uncanny frequency. The man could *smell* when we were low on inventory. We occasionally missed sales when we ran out of stock, but we rarely were stuck with outdated inventory. Or he would simply walk the aisles of the old warehouse and, through some magical osmosis, borne of years of experience in the trade, just *know* if a gross of sweatshirts had been mislabeled. My father was fastidious and intuitive about many things.

Occasionally, a customer wanted to return items long after the sale—not that there was anything wrong with the merchandise; the customer often ordered too many size mediums, for example, their evanescent profit margin disappearing if a few extra garments remained unsold. Ever the young lawyer, I would remind my father of our return policy—written on the back of each invoice—that precluded refunding the money if a customer did not act in a timely fashion. "Mine firstborn son, the last angry man," my father would tease. Invariably, my father would reach an accommodation with the customer and refund the money. At first, this would frustrate me, but DW taught me that any courtesy we extend to others is a down payment in the karmic bank of commerce.

Lesson Number 1: In my father's reckoning, life was too short to worry about small problems. "Steven, the refund won't make him rich, and it won't make us poor. There is more to life than this."

Nearly every day, we'd eat together. The meal consisted of brown bag lunches packed by my mother. I'd encourage my father to call up a friend for lunch, but he preferred to eat at his desk. I'd sit across from him, and like a magician of the old school, he'd peer into the paper bag and draw out . . . an orange . . . a peanut butter and jelly sandwich . . . a turkey sandwich . . . and best of all, last of all . . . red licorice! My father would begin by meticulously peeling the orange with his pen knife, quartering it with care and offering me the first slice, his own form of libation, in honor of his son.

It was a testament to my father's frugality and my mother's culinary originality that sometimes the sandwiches came out in unorthodox fashion: turkey, lettuce, and tomato on cinnamon-raisin toast. But my father always took delight in such inventive compromise. We'd have the same conversation every day, a Milwaukee version of Jack Lemmon and Walter Matthau: "Steverino, mine firstborn, what do you want, PB & J or turkey?" "You're the boss, you choose," I'd reply. "Let's split 'em, whaddya say?" The same conversation, same result, every day for three years. And every day, at every lunch, he'd conclude with a grin, "That Junie Cookie!" (His pet name for my mother.) "She's something special!"

Lesson Number 2: Take joy in the little things and give credit to those who pack your lunch—celebrate those who sustain you in ways both large and small.

DW would end each lunch by taking the aluminum foil from our sandwiches, folding it, neatly squaring the corners, and saving it to take home for the next day's lunch. My father's frugality was not centered solely on money, though he was a child of the Great Depression and a certain fiscal worry pervaded his psyche. He was no high roller. But his frugality was most significantly marked by an economy of speech, his ability to listen to others, his insistence on understanding disparate and often competing points of view, and to hold them both equally in his mind, in suspended animation—the mark, I think, of a true intellectual—before trying to reconcile them. He abhorred pomposity and intellectual bullying. He wore his education and his intellect lightly. He *listened*—rather than reacted—in order to better understand. When a smug salesman from one of the large mills in Alabama came to deliver the news that under a new quota system, we no longer qualified for "most favored nation" pricing unless we grew 40 percent in one year—a practical impossibility—my father was the picture of equanimity. DW explained that while he saw the mill's point of view, the inevitable consolidation of regional distributors would mean that, the mills, long accustomed to dictating terms of sale to a passel of obedient distributors, soon would find themselves beholden to the two or three largest national distributors—and did they really want such an outcome? Had the mills thought about that? And what need would the mills have of traveling salesmen if they had only three large, national customers they could service as inside house accounts?

Lesson Number 3: Don't get furious, get curious.

From my father, I inherited a knack for physics—especially the concept of a half-life, which is the interval required for a quantity of matter to decay to half of its initial value. In the cosmology of our family, the half-life concept usually centered on the last piece of sour cream coffee cake, a treasured family recipe from our Aunt Min, Monya Tolkan. Aunt Min had taught DW that it is the height of good manners to leave the last piece of coffee cake for someone else. That said, she saw nothing wrong in cutting the last piece in half and enjoying one of the halves—and continuing to halve the cake until only a sliver remained on the plate. Under Aunt Min's tutelage, DW became the Enrico Fermi of the kitchen table, surgically slicing the cake into ever-smaller halves, the David Wallace Theorem of Culinary Half-Lives. At last my mother in exasperation would throw a dish towel: "David, for crying out loud, just finish the ever-loving cake!" And sheepishly, he would answer, "I only wanted a bite." Then, with mock resignation—*if you insist*—he'd take the very last bite, smacking his lips and daubing the plate with the back of the fork to capture every crumb. He never lost this game with my mother in forty-eight years of marriage. From DW I learned how important it is to keep your spouse—that most valuable of stakeholders in any entrepreneurial venture—content and happy as possible. And if you do, your business often lives to see another day.

Lesson Number 4: There is an internal pace to every transaction, every negotiation; don't try to rush things. Be patient, play your role. Don't rush your lines, and you usually get what you want.

This rule applies in business, naturally, but one of my father's greatest planning triumphs came at the expense of my wife, Linda, who is a year and a half older than I am, a fact that gives rise to much teasing; it allows me to claim that I am her boy toy.

During the first year of my marriage to Linda, my father gave me one of those birthday cards recounting historical events that occurred during the year of your birth. Instead of using the correct 1961 card, he bought the 1962 card, effectively making me two and a half years younger than Linda. I opened the card, commented on the price of bread in 1962, and passed the card around the table. Linda, whose quick mathematical mind promptly discerned my age, looked at me, astonished and a little hurt.

"You said you were born in 1961. When were you really born?"

"1962," I lied.

Linda, the lawyer, whom my father had lovingly nicknamed "The Little General," flew into battle mode. "Where is your birth certificate? I want to see it now! Go get it." Now my father had *anticipated* this and prepared a copy of my real birth certificate, forging the 1962 date on it. He sulked out to his bedroom, fossicked about his desk for a believable interlude, and came back with my forged birth certificate. Linda examined the evidence, shrieked, and lit into the both of us before we could keep straight faces no longer and admitted the ruse, howling with laughter.

Lesson Number 5: Prepare, prepare, prepare—do your homework and anticipate what others are likely to do.

My father was not the type who single-mindedly focused on business to the exclusion of family, service to community, and his own intellectual well-being. He loved the theater, and two of his favorite characters were Tevye from *Fiddler on the Roof* and the King of Siam from *The King and I*. The characters have much in common, and the roles resonated profoundly for my father. Both are authority figures (one a papa and one a king), and both are compelled by history and circumstance to extend themselves, to test the tensile strength of their character, to find ways to adapt to a changing, bewildering world. Tevye can compromise only so far before disowning his daughter Chava, who marries outside the Jewish faith. The King of Siam struggles to modernize his country while simultaneously preserving the essence of his infallibility. Within months of my joining DW in the family business, it became clear that the unrelenting consolidation in the wholesale garment industry was going to require us to either sell or risk going out of business, as deep-pocketed competitors surgically undercut our prices and poached even our most loyal customers. A few years earlier, my father had radically reengineered the family sweater business into the present-day blank goods distributorship when faced with the demise of the small-town haberdashers who were the lifeblood of the old business. Much like Yaw Brobbey reallocating his capital

50

from farming yams to farming rabbits, DW possessed a remarkable capacity to adapt to his environment. DW was clear-eyed and largely unsentimental. This latest challenge, however, would ultimately prove insurmountable—no amount of pivoting could reverse the rising tide of industry consolidation in the wholesale T-shirt business. Midstates Sportswear had grown fast in the last two years, but not nearly fast enough. DW wandered into the sample room, arms outstretched, a Midwestern Yul Brynner, asking no one in particular, "Who is King?" Compromise is the defining attribute of emotional and psychological growth—it demonstrates your capacity to forgive and forget. My father bore no ill will toward the fast-growing, rapacious New Jersey distributor that had come into our market and so disrupted his congenial world. DW understood that the time had come to exit the rag trade, his economic well-being depended on it, but that's not to say it was easy to do. And yet, when it came time to sell, he embraced the moment with equanimity. On the last day he owned the business, we walked, for the final time, the long rows of the warehouse, turning out the aisle lights one by one. We reached the last aisle and he turned to me and said, "It's only T-shirts, Steverino. Let's leave it all to the mice."

Lesson Number 6: Know what's important. Discern what's not. Have the capacity to let go and understand that much of life is just not that important.

* * *

Technically speaking, you could say I had a corner office at Midstates Sportswear, but it was tucked in a corner of the windowless sample room. Often, at the end of the workday, I turned out the lights and put my head down on the teak conference table, a reminder of plummier days, back in the 1960s, when the family sweater business had a New York showroom in the Empire State Building. These days, the imposing table had been repurposed as a workspace where

I manually configured catalog layouts, using 3 x 5 index cards, Scotch tape, and bottles of Wite-Out.

The question on my mind wasn't *How best to showcase a raglan sleeve or a 3-button placket?* or *How can we increase sales by highlighting the wafflelike weave of our pique golf shirts?* No, if I were thinking about things like those, I'd be able to hold up my head. My overriding question was far weightier: *What am I going to do with the rest of my life?*

I stared blankly at the jigsaw puzzle of notecards on the conference room table—our upcoming catalog layout. Regardless of how I arranged the pages, the final chapter of Midstates Sportswear was already written. Brutal consolidation within our industry had revealed our Achilles heel: we lacked the capital to secure national distribution that would ensure our long-term viability by making us indispensable to the mills that supplied our shirts. These mills offered price discounts to their largest customers. If we couldn't grow sales, we'd have to pay more for our products than our larger competitors; and because our prices were just a bit higher, we'd continue to lose customers. We were in a death spiral. We were like the corner drugstore when Walgreen's came to town, a soon-to-be anachronism in a world of predictive analytics and perpetual inventories. Our best course of action was to ready the company for sale to a fast-growth competitor with national ambitions who wanted to expand into our Upper Great Lakes market. Sitting in the dark, in the sample room, I contemplated this, my second career false start. *Brilliant. Is this how it goes? Two strikes and I'm out? Is all this my fault—or that of a larger, tidal ebb and flow of the global economy?* Did it matter? My old law firm had no real succession plan and was losing young partners left and right. I had the good sense to exit before I devoted more years to a firm that held little future. For Midstates Sportswear, I added new customers while simultaneously cutting our marketing budget—but the inexorable industry consolidation meant midmarket firms like ours had to grow jaw-droppingly fast, sell to a competitor, or go bankrupt. I felt I was in a very small skiff, with but a single oar—lacking agency, in a turbulent, roiling economic ocean.

But something wouldn't allow me to dwell too long on that dismal topic, and now my thoughts again returned to Ghana, that country of wondrous enchantments. *No wonder I like to reminisce. My past is more interesting than my future.* And Ghana is a gallimaufry of great stories.

I closed my eyes and I was back in Sunyani, tucked into the back seat of Yaw Brobbey's Toyota after a day of traveling the back roads of Brong-Ahafo. We were driving home at night, the dirt road still radiating heat from the afternoon sun. As cozy as I felt, I knew even then that there was good reason to be fearful of auto accidents in Ghana. The prospect of death by vehicle far outweighed more exotic hazards such as malaria, political violence, or snakes. Ghanaian vehicles are often poorly maintained, though jerry-rigged in ingenious, resourceful ways. Many roads are in disrepair, riven with potholes and lacking adequate shoulders; often, there are no streetlights or traffic signals in rural areas. Emergency services back in 1978 were nonexistent outside of major cities.

My thoughts wandered to the last accident I'd seen in Ghana. It had been a doozy: a lorry overturned, windshield smashed, blood on the hood. The truck had been piled impossibly high with jute bags of cocoa beans making their way from Brong-Ahafo to the port at Tema, bound for export. Onlookers were stunned, unsure how best to pry the unconscious driver from the cab. One man appeared to be stealing the cargo, which now littered the road.

Still slumped over the conference table, I thought, almost dreamily, *Cocoa is a valuable commodity. Too bad Ghana hasn't found a way to make more of it.*

Suddenly, a light went on.

It was DW, standing by the light switch at the doorway. "I don't mind your saving money on the electric bill, Steverino, but I don't want you sitting in the dark, either. You'll ruin your eyes."

"DW, I just got an idea."

Ɛnyɛ da a wɔ dua bayerɛe no ara na wɔ si ne pam.
It is not on the same day that the yam seed is sown that the stick upon
which its stem will crawl is also affixed.

---

*"An ambitious task is not begun and completed
on the same day."*

CHAPTER 4

Chicken or Fish?

My first phone call to the Embassy of Ghana in Washington, DC, did not go well. I attributed the staff's diffidence to the fact that Ghana had once been a British colony known as the Gold Coast. I blame the British Monarchy for the institutional formality and unblinking adherence to bureaucratic procedure that met my first inquiries.

"Please, sir, what is your name again?"

I fought the impulse to raise my voice. We were struggling to understand our common English language. My broad Midwestern vowels and nasal intonation were as confounding, I feared, as my Ghanaian compatriot's rapid-fire delivery and dropping of the letter R. I'm sure he thought he spoke English *bettah* and *fastah* than I.

"My name is Steve. Steven Wallace."

"Ah, Steven Lawlor."

"No, Wallace."

"Steven Lawless."

"No, W-A-L-L-A-C-E. I'm trying to find out if there are any chocolate factories in Ghana. I'm thinking of building a chocolate factory in Ghana. I used to live in Sunyani."

"Ahaaaa. Mistah Steve. First, I will need to have you write me a letter. On your letterhead. You see?"

"Why a letter? Can't you just answer some questions now on the phone?"

I doctored up some company letterhead for the Wifely Sprockets Company, a nondescript name chosen to keep our intentions secret for as long as possible. My laughable conceit was that Cadbury's or Hershey's might beat me to market with a single-origin Ghana chocolate bar, so I wanted to disguise my purpose. Only in retrospect do I realize that the Wifely Sprockets name did me no favors in Ghana, a place whose ministries had little sense of humor. I put myself in a deputy minister's shoes: Would I want to associate with a chocolate company that didn't even have the word "chocolate" in its name? *What does this* obroni *mean by calling his company a sprocket company? What does a sprocket have to do with cocoa?* I might have helped myself if I'd thought that through—but I didn't.

And so, on Wifely Sprockets letterhead, I sent off a formal letter requesting information. Weeks later, a reply arrived, directing me simply to resubmit my request to Ghana's Embassy to the United Nations in New York, as that office had a staff member with private investment as part of his portfolio.

He replied—by letter—that I must write to someone else. Who in turn instructed me to write to someone else. And so on. There was no e-mail in 1991, and there was no progress in my epistolary quest: no response led to any advance. This went on for a year.

At last, after exchanging many letters with Ghana's US Embassy in Washington, DC, and its UN Embassy in New York, I reached out to the US Embassy in Accra. I figured that if Ghana wasn't so keen on the investment, perhaps the US Embassy would see some benefit from having an American private investor in-country. But the first-tier commercial and economic officers did not know quite what to do with my chocolate factory proposal. In retrospect, I can hardly blame them, as the proposal came from a company with a confounding name and was headed by a former tax attorney who had never sold a single chocolate bar in his entire life; moreover, he had zero experience running a cocoa-processing factory.

Since the Embassy could not simply ignore a written request from a tax-paying US citizen (*thank goodness for bureaucratic procedures . . .*), my file passed down the chain of command until it landed on the desk of Michael J. "Cogs" Caughlin, a United States Agency for International Development (USAID) staffer in Washington, DC, who worked with that agency's resident office in Accra. "Cogs" had curiously bested the mandatory two-year rotation system of the diplomatic corps, designed to prevent staffers from becoming too close to their host country and perhaps susceptible to local influence-peddling. After a brief stay in Washington, Cogs was about to return for an unprecedented second extension of his original tour of duty in his beloved Ghana. I would soon learn that his maverick style got more done, in less time, than anyone else in the entire mission that included USAID, the Embassy proper, and the Peace Corps—and I sensed he had the institutional enemies in each agency to prove it. Yet it was not my intent to run the chocolate company as an aid project. My plan was to create an arm's-length, for-profit, sustainable business; it puzzled me that my proposal found its way to USAID, the arm of the US government concerned with international humanitarian aid.

Even over the phone, it was obvious Cogs possessed a gregarious sociability—part singing cowboy, part fraternity rush chairman. He did not fit my preconceived notion of a diplomat responsible for foreign-aid projects. Cogs would chuckle at something I said and then turn deadly serious, his soft drawl leading me to suspect he was a man with a mysterious past. Over time I would see that Cogs loved hijinks and seemed to have a gravitational affinity for finding trouble. He was a man with magpie interests, and on one occasion in Ghana, he insisted on stopping the car and snapping photos of a strange-looking bird—a bird that alighted on the security wall of what turned out to be a top-secret Government of Ghana facility. He was detained by the Ghanaian police, who did not buy for a moment his earnest bird-watching story. His insouciance for authority made me wonder how he'd succeeded for so long in his peripatetic career—one that included stints in the Green Berets, the Department of Agriculture's Foreign Agriculture Service, and, finally, USAID. Of course, I wondered if he might not be CIA—that would explain perhaps, his extended tour of duty in Ghana. Like many Vietnam veterans, Cogs possessed an abiding hope that *this* time perhaps his government might get something right and help someone, some-place, for the good of the US and for the good of the world.

Within a year, Cogs became my tactical team leader, father con-fessor, and sage guide through the impenetrable sea of acronyms that is the lingua franca of any bureaucracy, especially that of the US government. He could deconstruct a government regulation or agency funding initiative with the inventiveness of any K Street tax lawyer back in Washington, DC. He could uncover previously unavailable dollars or neatly sidestep, with balletic skill, a burden-some legal requirement. I'm certain most of his superiors found him a colossal pain in the ass. But most importantly, Cogs embraced lost causes. And my chocolate factory was certainly beginning to look like a lost cause.

After several months of exchanging letters and phone calls, Cogs told me it was time for me to come to Ghana and, with the help of one of his staffers, see what progress we could make. He was due to fly over on other business, and he invited me to meet him there. I hadn't been back to Ghana since 1978, and I was trying to save money by postponing my first trip until it was clear my plan had some likelihood of success. My wife and I had twins barely a year old. Money was tight. But Cogs and I had exhausted all we could do from a distance.

Cogs told me that I would have the help of his right-hand man in Accra, a Ghanaian, Daniel Gyimah. Daniel was an FSN, a Foreign

Service National (young Ghanaians in their mid-thirties who displayed unusual talent and were appointed to two-year stints with the US Embassy in Accra). FSNs represented a long-term bet—they were people with whom the US government wanted to build a relationship, in the hope they might rise to take leadership positions in Ghanaian politics or industry. In the short term, from what I could discern, the Embassy used FSNs as "fixers" to get things done in Ghana's bewildering cultural and political landscape.

Cogs and Daniel had developed an extraordinary relationship, and I could see that Daniel loved working with Cogs. Cogs was "the rare American who knows how to play the game in Ghana," Daniel told me, and together we marveled at the way Cogs could push, cajole, shame, and compliment, all in one breath. At the same time, Cogs valued Daniel, and I observed that it took a rare sort of diplomat to realize that a hotshot with an advanced degree from a fancy School of Advanced International Studies would be simply no match for a resourceful thirty-six-year-old Ghanaian with gumption, wit, and a few connections. Cogs wisely determined that, if these FSNs were to reap results, they required a good deal more freedom from supervision than you would otherwise demand of your own career foreign service officers.

Daniel's sincerity of purpose and love of country meant that he often played the straight man to Cogs's antics. Taking great pride in his roots, Daniel often appeared at official functions in full traditional robes and leather sandals, something of an anomaly in modern Accra. He bore the weight of high expectations from his family, his Akan ethnic group, and his nation. Daniel, for his part, delighted in Cogs's freewheeling approach, even though it nearly always left Daniel to clean up the mess, like bailing Cogs out of a Ghanaian jail for taking unauthorized photos of a singularly feathered bird.

As it turned out, Daniel grew up in Sunyani. As far as I was concerned, this meant that we were practically related—*two Sunyani boys*—surely a stroke of good fortune. Daniel even knew Yaw Brobbey very well; they attended the same Catholic church.

"I expect that Sunyani was like nothing you had ever seen, when you were a boy," Daniel said to me once. "Ghana is not Wisconsin."

"I was disoriented from the minute I arrived," I replied. It occurred to me to tell him how I disembarked from the plane, getting reprimanded by the flight attendant and winding up on the front page of the newspaper. I hadn't even finished telling the story before Daniel started to laugh. He asked me to repeat exactly what I did as I disembarked. I stood up and mimed the gesture of tying my windbreaker around my waist.

"Oh, Steven! That is *too* much!" Daniel laughed, emphasizing the word "too," an emphatic used throughout Ghana. "That is *too* funny! Ei! When you adjust your robe about your waist, it is regarded as getting ready to fight an enemy—you are girding your loins. It is a sign of aggression from a warrior! Ha! I can't believe you did this on your first day in Ghana. Steven, you are *too* funny."

"I was just hot."

At long last I realized that it had taken me all of ten seconds to offend the country that would be my new home. And my transgression had been there for all to see, on the cover of the *Ghanaian Times* in the summer of 1978.

* * *

The Labadi Beach Hotel, in 1992, was the nicest hotel in all of Ghana. The low, two-story building boasted dark wood railings, broad verandas, a tranquil swimming pool, and an abundance of charm. The Labadi's lobby bar was the favorite haunt of spies both corporate and government, deal seekers, information traders, diamond merchants, brokers of gold, and dealers in cocoa.

I had come to the Labadi to meet Michael Caughlin face-to-face for the first time. I walked the length of the second-story veranda, where all the fanciest rooms are. *Surely this can't be right.* I double-checked the room number and knocked on the mahogany door. A uniformed Ghanaian porter peered out, bowing slightly. From behind him, I heard a voice calling, "Jes' a minute, Steven"—a hint of a drawl. No one at home calls me Steven, it's always "Steve," and I immediately brightened at the formality of his greeting. A hint of jocularity infused his address, as if Cogs might be playacting. I peeked in.

Cogs had his hands on the porter's shoulders and looked him straight in the eyes. "Now, Kwame," Cogs said softly, like an avuncular junior varsity football coach, "I want you to bring me a bucket of ice, very full, very cold." He turned and handed the porter an ice bucket. "Fill this to the brim. And some bottled water. No gas. *Still.* You've got this, right?"

The porter looked overwhelmed.

"And get me some limes. Six limes. That's my good man!"

Coming from anyone else, this pantomime would smack of the most wince-inducing sort of cultural insensitivity. But I would come to learn that Cogs *loved*—and that is not too strong a word for it—the people of Ghana like few foreigners I've ever met. Cogs pressed some filthy cedis—in 1992 all cedis bore the grime of innumerable hands and were soft as ring-spun cotton—into the porter's hand.

"Yes, sir!" Kwame saluted, deftly palming the notes as he bounded out the door.

"Steven, enter!"

Cogs stood before me, in a bathrobe, bare-legged and bare everything else underneath, I guessed. Somehow he had procured the presidential suite for himself, though his government per diem would barely cover the cost of a single room. No doubt he worked his charm with the desk clerk and likely everyone else at the hotel, including the porter who now served as his personal butler. On a small table sat a leather attaché case that in actuality was a travel bar, with compartments for a bottle of scotch and bottle of gin, a silver jigger, and a set of four cut-glass crystal tumblers. Cogs offered me a drink and beamed in a way that reminded me of Yaw Brobbey, offering me scotch first thing in the morning.

"Tomorrow we'll go to the USAID office, but Daniel will be here shortly. He's been setting up some meetings for you." I brightened at the news.

Finally, I thought, *progress!* I had arrived in Ghana with not much more than my enthusiasm and a fifty-seven-page Memorandum of Understanding, a carefully crafted document into which I poured every ounce of skill I had gleaned from my days at the law firm. I thought now would be a good time to pull out that prized document, in case Cogs wanted to go over details. He pushed the memo aside and put his tumbler on it, using it as a coaster.

He leaned forward conspiratorially. "Your chocolate factory idea," he whispered, choosing his words carefully, stroking his chin, "is just what these fuckers should have been doing for years. Just march straight up the value chain, and leave the bean trading to the idiots in the Ivory Coast."

Cogs loved almost everything about Africa—but he played favorites, and Ghana was at the top of his list, his haloed child. He saw something just a tad subversive about my nascent company, with its contrarian story that Ghana could be home to a luxury food product like chocolate. My idea presented a not-so-subtle challenge to the paternalistic marketing campaigns of many organizations that sought to portray Ghana as an economically poor country filled with sick people, deserving of charity. I counted myself lucky that my quirky, for-profit chocolate factory idea was now supported by USAID's rogue staffer, who likewise wanted desperately to tell the story of a new, emergent, ascendant Ghana.

Daniel arrived. He bore a striking resemblance to the actor Yaphet Kotto, and he glowed, as if whatever he'd been doing this morning had gone exceptionally well. I fought off the effects of jet lag and gin long enough to ask him what kinds of meetings he'd set up for me.

"It's time," Cogs declared, pausing for effect, "to kiss some frogs."

Daniel nodded in agreement.

"You gotta get out and pound the pavement. Meet every assistant deputy minister that will take a meeting, have a beer with all the bankers and the people here who make this town *run*. You gotta find your fairy princess. Pucker up. Daniel will help."

So started the first of many trips back to Ghana as I puckered up and started kissing frogs. Daniel set up a meeting with Prosper Opoku, a Ghanaian who had made his fortune first in the timber industry and then manufacturing cutlasses, the ubiquitous Ghanaian steel machetes used for everything from slicing pineapples to splitting cocoa pods. Opoku reputedly made a cedi on every single one. He wanted me to see his latest venture, a rehabilitation of an old Firestone rubber plantation at Cape Three Points, the southernmost tip of Ghana.

I was dressed as inappropriately as could be, in a navy suit and tie and a pair of Allen Edmonds wing tips, for a hike in the tropics. Prosper forbade me to dirty my shoes and insisted that his driver carry me piggyback for thirty-five minutes through the plantation, in what counts as one of my most humiliating experiences in Ghana—or anywhere, for that matter. Afterward, Opoku drove me to his house, where we took off our shoes, Japanese-style, and sat on pillows while a servant wheeled in a chrome bar cart stacked with Johnnie Walker Black, Courvoisier, Tanqueray, and a host of other top-shelf liquors from abroad—costing Prosper a small fortune, I surmised. We talked of spirituality: the living room featured a painting of a Tibetan mandala, a weaving of Jesus with arms outstretched, and, most prominently, a wall-sized painting of the Buddha framed in plastic roses.

"You have a lovely home," I said, as I sipped a Tanqueray and tonic.

"Thank you, it actually belongs to one of my wives."

Welcome back to Ghana, I thought.

Had I been away too long? Back at my hotel, I reached for my copy of Emmanuel Ekuban's definitive Twi grammar. A slim volume, it nevertheless accommodates such curious phrases as "Lie supine on the floor." I was not sure why I would need to say this, but Mr. Ekuban at least told me *how* to say it: *"Da ayenya wɔ fam hɔ!"* I also consulted C. A. Akrofi's definitive modern collection of Twi *Mmebusɛm,* or proverbs. "Proverbs play a very important part in the everyday language of Twi-speaking people," Akrofi wrote. "Indeed, in Akan society, skill in the use of proverbs is a hallmark of good breeding."

Good breeding, yes, and the key to understanding how this culture operates on so many levels. My father had taught me always to prepare, and I knew I had homework to do.

Later, I found myself walking the furrows of a cocoa farm for the first time since my days in Sunyani. Daniel had arranged for me to meet Ian Stoddard, an American who years ago had befriended the man who would later become head of state. Stoddard married a Ghanaian woman, and cultivated what was reputedly the largest single cocoa farm in all of Ghana.

I also met Edmund "Kofi" van der Puije, the director of a small brokerage firm that would later expand to become the Dow Jones of Ghana; Dr. Clement Amega, the chief botanist with CRIG, the Cocoa Research Institute of Ghana, the government-run agronomy station located in Tafo established back in colonial times; Paa Gyamfi Adu, the chief economist in Ghana's Ministry of Finance; and Charity Lartey, a Baker Scholar from the Harvard Business School, recently returned to Ghana from a high-flying career with Goldman Sachs, now running her own investment firm, First African National Securities, Ltd. Making these appointments proved nearly impossible. It would be five years until mobile phones entered the market. Land-line phones were unreliable, motorway traffic was oppressive, and if you were lucky enough to secure a meeting in advance, schedules often ran late. I refused to quit.

So many meetings, so many frogs. But not one princess.

* * *

Then one day Daniel introduced me to a young Ghanaian, Kojo Quist Bamford, who was struggling to turn around his family's aluminum fabrication business. Kojo's company crafted doorframes and windows. He was Ghana-skinny and sported muttonchops and a wee beard. Impatient, he spoke of bold plans: factories and automation and remaking entirely the customer experience in Africa. Kojo was skeptical of Americans, and yet fascinated by them. He was ambitious in the best sense of the word, contemptuous of bureaucrats (though, ironically, his father was one of the highest-ranking bureaucrats in the old colonial administration). Above all, Kojo was undaunted by the challenge of building a business from the ground up.

We met for drinks in the lobby bar of the Labadi Hotel. I confess the particulars of our first encounter remain vague. I don't drink much, and the equatorial heat and oppressive humidity of the Accra Plain rendered alcohol even more potent. I recall we both postured a bit: Kojo demonstrating how well he knew Sacramento and Lake Tahoe, how he could both laugh and despair at Ghanaian culture with an expatriate's ease. And yet there was a poignant pride. I countered with Sunyani stories, artfully (I hoped) dropping Twi phrases into the conversation.

Kojo told me that growing up, he had no Ghanaian entrepreneurial role models—no one at all like Yaw Brobbey. Really, Kojo said, among the older generation, the self-made, independent Yaw Brobbey was an outlier, a lone wolf, a survivor; he was an entrepreneur before that word held any currency at all. Even among Kojo's contemporaries, most aspired to a comfortable sinecure in a sprawling government bureaucracy.

So Kojo represented the first wave of Ghanaian entrepreneurs, many of whom founded and lost businesses during the lost decades when coup after coup betrayed the promise of Nkrumah's Black Star of Africa. Nevertheless, Kojo displayed an implacability in the face of repeated disappointment and financial distress. Kojo's generation of expatriate returnees gave up a life of ease in London or the US for a life of hardship in Accra—and did so when there was no assurance that things might improve politically or economically. It is no surprise that there were damn few willing to take this risk.

As a result, Kojo had little patience with the latest wave of expatriate arrivistes. "They come here fresh from McKinsey or Goldman Sachs, and they expect modern Ghana to welcome them back with a high-profile consulting job, equity options, and the six-figure incomes they enjoyed in New York or London." Kojo shook his head. "Steve, this place is *hard*. . . . *Seriously*. You better be prepared."

Kojo had an American wife, Janice, whom he had met in California. Kojo had a Golden Ticket—he could have, if he had chosen, become a US citizen and stayed in the US. But he never wanted that. He did enjoy the generosity of the US Embassy, at least for the annual Fourth of July reception at the Ambassador's residence, and he made a habit of meeting Americans passing though Ghana, always in the hope that some business relationship might blossom. Kojo and I were about the same age and were the products of doting mothers who had high expectations for their first-born sons. In short, we sprang from the same fertile petri dish that has spawned so many entrepreneurs the world over.

More meetings, more drinks. A lot more talk. Kojo took me under his wing, gave me the use of his car and driver, and helped set up meetings at the ministries, though it was difficult to discern what ministry was responsible for a private investment in the cocoa sector. The Ghana Cocoa Board? Certainly. The Ministry of Trade and Industry? Evidently, yes. The Ministry of Employment and Labor Relations? They wanted their say. The Ministry of Food and Agriculture? Arguably, yes. It was slow work.

Why was it so hard to make progress within the ministries of Accra? Almost no one I met possessed anything like an entrepreneurial vision—which meant it was impossible for them to understand my own. *A man like Yaw Brobbey would back my proposal,* I thought. But how did Yaw Brobbey emerge as such a talented entrepreneur up in Sunyani, far from Ghana's capital city? Was there some rural vs. urban divide at work?

I believe there was. The fertile soil of rural Ghana gave rise not only to the propagation of premium cocoa, but also to generations of entrepreneurs, small stakeholder farmers who chose to grow a cash crop destined for export rather than a subsistence crop, like yams or cassava. These farmers understood both the precariousness and the opportunities inherent in serving a global supply chain. While Brong-Ahafo and the Central Region were home to such agricultural entrepreneurs, the cities were less fortunate and couldn't offer comparable opportunities. Stroll down the smaller streets in urban Ghana, and you will find more storefront churches than merchants—more prayer than payroll. And as Kojo had already explained to me, the dearth of entrepreneurial role models like Yaw Brobbey had legacy consequences—which in turn had consequences for me.

* * *

I had plenty of time to consider my lack of progress, I tried to put myself in a Ghanaian deputy minister's shoes. Government ministries are inherently risk-averse institutions. They need to be. They have a fiduciary responsibility to safeguard public resources; they certainly have no mandate to act as venture investors. Due to its colonial history, with a managed economy, Ghana remained a high-ly-regulated environment whose large public sector spread into many corners of daily life. Government was seemingly everywhere, and because of this broad reach it compelled private industry to cooperate. Here lay the irony: while Ghana's government eagerly sought private investment, the long legacy of government intervention was hardly inviting to investors. If I wanted to work in the cocoa sector, I couldn't ignore government. But I tried diligently to understand its point of view. Despite their advanced degrees from the London School of Economics, Oxford, or Wharton, no minister wanted anything to do with a new venture that carried with it even the remote possibility of failure. I knew start-up food businesses in the US had a failure rate of something like 90 percent. The odds in Ghana, I imagined, were even worse. It wasn't a question *if* my chocolate factory might *conceivably* fail—my plan was almost certain *to fail.* Only I didn't yet appreciate this fact. I could hardly blame people for avoiding me.

"Steven, don't think too much about getting permission," Kojo upbraided me after one meeting with a deputy minister. "Just make small progress. Ei! What do you want this gent to do? He is an old man, he is five years away from his pension! He is done. Finished! *Finito!* Do not expect him to embrace new ideas! You must know better."

Of course, ministerial bureaucrats were risk-averse. In Ghana in the early 1990s, the only viable employment was a government job. In 1992, some 85 percent of all Ghanaians worked for the government. *Eighty-five percent!* The Ghana Cocoa Board alone employed some 43,000 workers, and if you screwed up as Chief Executive of the Ghana Cocoa Board, 42,999 people were gunning for your job. The private sector was practically nonexistent. The pressure to conform to the ministerial status quo demanded that you avoid—at all costs—any decision that might bear even the faintest whiff of potential failure.

I needed to kiss some more frogs.

Still, I had learned two valuable lessons. First, when too many people are in charge, *nobody* is in charge. It's not that every ministry wanted to take the lead on my project—just the opposite—for that would mean taking responsibility for potential failure, and for that reason alone, no ministry wanted to formally endorse the Omanhene project. But each ministry did want to be consulted, be included in the conversation, on the off chance that Omanhene might find success. Yet, within this passive-aggressive no-man's-land, in those small interstices where the Ghana Cocoa Board brushed elbows with the Ministry of Trade and Industry, for example, I might find room enough to proceed. It's not a blue-ocean strategy so much as it is a chocolate-*sliver* strategy. I didn't need a lot of room to maneuver, just a little space where we might operate out of direct sight of the ministries and the multinationals that dominated the world of cocoa processing. "Don't think too much about permission." Kojo's advice was beginning to make sense. I decided that we would proceed with or without signed permission, with or without my signed Memorandum of Understanding. I would bear full responsibility for the failure of the Omanhene project. And if we were to succeed, I recognized that I generously would have to share the success with every ministry where I had sat waiting for hours, for the simple courtesy of a meeting.

The second lesson was, many senior Ghanaian officials, with the weight of a nation upon them—and the promise of a pension ahead of them—were risk-averse in the extreme. Long years of avoiding large strategic decisions with potentially painful consequences had rendered them impotent to make even small ones. It was a wonder they could decide between the meat or fish entree when flying business class on Ghana Airways.

I shared this observation with Kojo's wife, Janice. We were well into our second bottle of Rondebosch, a fine South African red, lying supine on their veranda, munching on fried plantains dipped in the salty shrimp sauce known locally as *shito*. Janice adored this image of government officials on the plane. She set down her glass, stood up, and swished about the couch, pretending to be a surly Ghana Airways flight attendant, barking orders at Kojo and me, her make-believe passengers.

"Chicken or fish? Chicken or fish? Honorable, hurry up, please, I haven't got all day! Can't you see I've an entire DC-10 to serve? Ei! What is taking you so long? It is a simple question-o. Chicken or fish? Chicken or fish? What will it be, sir, *what will it be*?"

Akɔkono de brɛ brɛ na ɛwe abɛ.

Though the grub in the palm tree is tiny, it can devastate the tree.

"However modest a person, great things can be achieved by perseverance and industry."

CHAPTER 5

The Waiting Game

I lost count of how many hallways and outer offices I had seen on this trip. I took up the habit of driving to a ministry, any ministry, walking the tranquil terrazzo corridors until I found the office of the person I wanted to see, and then I just waited until they agreed to meet with me. This was often a humiliating exercise. Sometimes I sat for hour, only to be told at long last that there was someone else in another office or another ministry whom I needed to meet instead.

One afternoon, the heat was rising in the anteroom of the office of the Deputy Minister of Trade and Industry. How did the British colonials survive this climate in the days before air conditioning?

An *obroni*—me—sat impassively, waiting without an appointment. An *obroni* of singular stubbornness, so it seemed to the Deputy Minister's secretary. An *obroni* tone deaf to certain unmistakable cultural cues. *"Ei! Why does he not leave? What is wrong with him? Can't he see that he is making me—making all of us here—so uncomfortable? Tsk, tsk, everyone needs an appointment-o."*

Next to me sat a watery-eyed man wearing *adinkra* cloth and stiff maroon-leather sandals, his head bowed as if in meditation, conserving his energy in the torpor. I bet he was a shirttail relative from the Minister's village, waiting for some handout to solve an intractable village problem.

I could wait longer than he can.

I could also wait longer than the young, smartly dressed woman with the Coach handbag sitting across from me, her firm thighs on full display. Bet she gets past the secretary before anyone else—mistress's privilege, I surmised.

The Deputy Minister's secretary, a young woman, busied herself with a newspaper bearing the headline, Fetish Priest Sez: "I did not bonk my sister!" She told me twice already, in the hope I would deferentially depart, that I didn't have an *appointment-o* and the Minister was quite busy today.

"Thank you, I intend to wait."

I would be leaving Ghana in a couple of days, I explained, and I couldn't seem to get the honorable Minister's office to confirm any sort of meeting. Of course, I did my best to make an appointment, but the landline telephones work sporadically, if at all, and when they do the combination of static and the dueling accents made conversation nearly impossible. We would shout hurried salutations into the receivers, and then our apologies, never entirely sure we understood the person at the other end of the line.

My letters and faxes went unanswered, though no doubt carefully filed away in sheaves of correspondence lining the walls—each sheaf bound in the ubiquitous pale-blue, government-issued construction paper, the pages secured with hand-knotted twine. Every ministerial anteroom, every provincial administration office, was lined with such paper binders. Daniel Gyimah told me that each incoming correspondence was given a code number, and every outgoing letter references the incoming code. Paper binder upon paper binder collected slowly falling motes of dust in the rising afternoon heat. All this correspondence, all this record-keeping, and yet I couldn't secure an appointment. I mentally graded this ministry:

Filing of records in blue binders: A+
Substantive progress in service to the nation: Incomplete

So I had come to sit, on this, my first trip back to Ghana since my Sunyani days. I sat, relearning a discipline as severe as the *zazen* practiced by a Buddhist acolyte.

Just a few days ago, I was buoyant at the prospect of establishing the first origin-based, bean-to-bar chocolate company focused exclusively on export markets. Introductions were made. Meetings taken. Now I was chopfallen as the full, dead weight of the endeavor settled about my shoulders.

Ghana was still under military rule. Flight Lieutenant Jerry Rawlings retained power but committed to multiparty elections in November of 1992, just a few weeks away. Would Ghanaians finally realize their postcolonial dream of democratic government? Would Ghana break the succession of military dictators and coups that had turned the 1960s, '70s, and '80s into the "lost decades"? Would Rawlings truly transition peacefully from coup-leader to a presidential candidate? Would his opposition cause trouble?

Would I *ever* get to see this minister?

No telling.

I knew this much: Sunyani taught me patience. So I could outlast my two companions and anyone else who wanted to join us here in the anteroom. Back in Sunyani, the tranquility of those who wait used to confound me. I once waited for a lumbering green State Transport Corporation bus to take me from Sunyani to Kumasi; it was four hours late. There was no bus depot or any way for those of us in line to know if the bus would ever show up *at-TALL*. It might have broken down. It might have crashed. But the people waiting for the bus displayed equanimity, complacency, and good humor, readjusting their robes every so often and shifting their weight from sandal to sandal as the hours passed. Even though I was just a kid, I began composing a letter in my head, mentally addressing the head of the State Transport Corporation—indicting the Corporation's lack of customer service and poor communications, a response so typically American in its sanctimony that I cringe to recall it even now.

A functionary in short sleeves and a narrow tie popped in the anteroom door, regarded the scene in a glance, committed an involuntary double take upon seeing an *obroni*, and nodded respectfully. "Hi, boss!" he said brightly, raising his hand in mock salute. I saluted back. He ignored the two others.

The phone rang, and the secretary answered it with uncharacteristic speed—grateful, perhaps, for something to do other than shoot me angry looks. Cradling the receiver on her shoulder, she looked at me now without a hint of embarrassment and nodded, speaking in Twi.

"Yes, sir. Ah, ha . . . ah, ha . . ." More rapid-fire Twi. "No, he *won't* go. Mmmm. Not *at-TALL*. He is just sitting-o. Mmmmmm." Click.

I knew the Deputy Minister was inside. He had arrived, I saw, just a few moments before I did, his large black Mercedes-Benz rolling up to the front of the Ministry to drop off this surprisingly diminutive gent with a likeable mien. Such a big, serious car for so slight a man—a man whose resume included past chairmanship of the Committee in Defense of the Revolution, the much-feared goon squad that specialized in suppressing opponents of Jerry Rawlings's first coup. Indeed, the Deputy Minister is an uncle of Jerry Rawlings. Years later, it would be alleged that the CDR handcuffed people and pushed them out of helicopters over the ocean, that the CDR publically flogged *makola* (market) women. This morning I watched the Deputy Minister share a laugh with his driver and smile at the junior clerks as he walked into the building. He looked anything but the strong-man type.

At some point, I told myself, the Deputy Minister would *have* to leave his office, and I would corner him in his anteroom if I had to. I

could follow him down the terrazzo corridor back to his car. I could
. . . *block his way*. I could be a tough guy, too.

Four miserable hours I had waited. My practiced calm gave way
to impatience, and my impatience to anger, which in turn gave way
to humiliation as I realized the Minister knew damn well I was waiting to see him. I checked my watch. I had an appointment later this
afternoon—the only actual appointment with a government official
that I could confirm ahead of time. It was with a special advisor to
the Head of State.

I agreed to meet with her in the Castle, not so very far away, but
the traffic in Accra was formidable and I like to be early, a point of
personal pride. I weighed the likelihood of getting to see the Deputy
Minister against keeping my appointment with the Special Advisor,
while at the same time trying to compute how the political hierar-
chy here worked. Who wielded more power? Which was the more
important meeting? I considered why the Deputy Minister, the Head
of State's political fixer, was only given the job of deputy minister
instead of the top spot of full minister. It did not yet occur to me that
being minister means being too much in the public spotlight, while
a deputy minister can go about business just outside the unrelenting
gaze of the media and civil society NGOs. A deputy minister can
work his private side deals in peace and relative quiet.

Four hours of waiting. My humiliation rose. If I left now, I failed.
And it would be a public failure. The self-satisfied secretary would
win. The Deputy Minister would win. *Adinkra*-man would smile
knowingly and probably chuckle as I headed out the door. The mistress? Well, she cared not a piffle for me. I wasn't her type; I wasn't
rich and I wasn't powerful. But hardest to swallow, *I would know* I
had failed—to hell with whoever else knew.

I was no closer to launch than I was before I arrived in Ghana.
For all the excitement, no one had expressed any willingness to do
anything concrete to help. No one wanted to support *yet another*
project from abroad, brimming with naive enthusiasm and doomed

to failure. One more precious, precocious young American with a breathtakingly ambitious business plan and copious, incontrovertible quantitative analyses. Charity with charts.

When that self-pity starts, it accelerates fast, baby.

So fast, that it gave me whiplash. I snapped out of my funk almost as quickly as I succumbed to it. What was wrong with me, anyway? *I can bear this humiliation. I've borne worse.* What if the Ghanaians didn't act in what I perceived to be their national self-interest? I simply would have failed to convince them otherwise. And I didn't need help from the US government; I would rather do this at arm's length. Do it myself. I probably knew more about how Ghana works than many of the development consultants. *I lived in Sunyani. I lived through a coup. I was up-country in 1978, when things were damn tough. My host father had three wives. Twenty-one children. I had amoebic dysentery. Ha!*

Chess time. I needed to decide. Stay or go? Head vs. heart? Chicken or fish?

I gathered up my briefcase and rose deliberately, as if I were in no hurry at all.

"Are you leaving, sir?" asked the secretary with feigned surprise and the galling suggestion of regret.

"Tell His Excellency that I'm sorry, but I have to go."

"Yes, sir." A look of relief spread across her face.

"I may try again later. Right now, though, I have an appointment at the Castle."

"Oh! The Castle? Yes, sir. Have a *very* good afternoon, sir." She picked up her phone and began to chatter in Twi to the Deputy Minister, concern in her voice. I heard her say something about "The Castle" as I politely closed the anteroom door.

Kojo Bamford had lent me the use of his Nissan Patrol and the services of his driver, Joshua, who played religious sermons full volume on the car radio. The Ghanaian preacher was screaming through the speakers, imploring sinners to repent and to follow Jesus Christ, our Redeemer, as I climbed back in. If piety equaled volume, all Ghana would be saved. Imprecations in Twi were followed by dramatically enunciated bits of English: "*Wo se, wo, homowo akyema kropong*, SUB-MISS-ION-TO-HIS-HO-LY-SPI-RIT, *fofo aboah se tsk, tsk. Ah haaaaaaaa . . .*"

"The Castle, please, Joshua," I said, the delicious majesty of this request hitting home.

* * *

Men love the trappings of office. Women seem embarrassed by them. By now I've seen so many governmental offices, I feel as if I've done field research for a dissertation. The décor varies from office to office, naturally, but what really distinguishes one from another isn't wealth or power. It's chromosomes. It's almost as if the size and furnishings of an office in Ghana bear an inverse relationship to the power wielded by the inhabitant. Most of the powerful women I've met in Ghana are happy with a modest work space. Few mementos, bare walls. A simple, almost Scandinavian aesthetic.

The men, on the other hand, have pictures of themselves shaking hands with various dignitaries, cheaply framed photos often strewn about without much thought or organization. Here, a credenza crenellated with a row of transaction mementoes encased in acrylic. Perhaps a signed soccer ball. There, a bookcase with a plastic model of a British Airways 747, shoved behind framed photos of children, the outside starboard engine broken off. The walls groan with the jumbled certificates of every short-term management course they have ever attended, as well as the obligatory portrait of the Head of State, a promotional calendar from Fan Milk or Accra Breweries Ltd., and quite often a portrait of a curiously white-skinned, smiling Jesus, as if from a 1950s schoolbook, framed garishly in silver plastic.

The Special Advisor, Akosua Nduom, rose to greet me. On her desk sat a jelly jar, wrapped in colored yarn (a kindergarten art project?) holding a wooden ruler and a half-dozen sharpened pencils. Everything else was government issue, unadorned. As I looked around the room, I understood: Akosua Nduom wasn't here to impress anybody. She didn't need to. She was here to *work*. In Ghana, proximity equals power, and her office was located right in the Castle, the official residence of the Head of State. I'd made the right choice by coming here, instead of continuing my lonely vigil in the Deputy Minister's anteroom.

This was the first time I'd been inside the Castle, a former slave fort built in the 1600s by the Danes, the most improbable slavers of them all, who called it Christiansborg Castle. Akosua's office faced the sea and had one small open window, no more than a slit really, just big enough for the barrel of an arquebus. The Castle was constructed to withstand assault from both land and sea. I would soon determine if it could withstand assault from within.

But there was little need for me to second-guess. First, Akosua had confirmed our appointment by phone, a nicety so rare in Ghana at that time that I was ready to hug her at first meeting. She'd done her homework when we spoke, and she knew a good bit about my work to date, confiding straightaway over the phone that "Ghana should be making chocolate for the whole world. Let us see what we can do."

Akosua cut an imposing figure. Formidable in her locally printed batik dress, her face could go from serious to smiling in a heartbeat. She was the sort who could tote up a column of numbers in her head faster than you, and then offer gentle correction when you came up with the wrong sum. Intimidated, I addressed her as "your excellency" when she invited me to take a seat.

"Oh, I'm not an excellency!" she said with a grin. "I have a special advisory role. Please, there is no need. I hope I can be of help to you, Mr. Steven Wallace."

Instinctively I could tell she was a product of one of the elite boarding schools in Ghana. If I had to guess, it would be Wesley Girls High School, from which so many political and business leaders have graduated. Our conversation flowed easily, businesslike yet warm. No need for false airs or pretense. *Wesley Girls, almost certainly*, I thought. Akosua promised to assist me. This woman clearly did not traffic in frivolity for the sake of easing conversation, but her economy of speech invested what she *did* say with great value—her word was her bond. As I rose to leave, I decided to test my cultural acuity, given that we had accomplished much and . . . well, I *liked* her. She had been so straightforward, with none of the artifice that seems to choke most conversation with male politicians. But I was careful, respectful, always respectful. I knew my place after all; I was still the small boy, and she the strict, if kindly, headmistress. Truth told, I wanted to show off a bit, so certain was I that I would be correct.

"Wesley Girls?" I asked.

"How did you know?" She seemed pleasantly surprised. She might even have thought, *Damned clever, this* obroni. I hoped so.

I placed my hands palms up in front of me and canted my head: *As if there were any other option*. "Wesley Girls run Ghana. Full stop."

She beamed.

Graduates of Wesley Girls wield power effectively and undertake the burdens of leadership with competence and sincerity of purpose. They excel at running sprawling, complex organizations like ministries and international NGOs. They know how to get things done. Underlings thrive working for them. They are closers. Graduates of Holy Child High School are equally accomplished but excel in the arts and in writing and education, more than in business or government. Achimota girls, by virtue of that school's coeducational student body, lack the particularly distaff comportment so unique to Wesley Girls; "Mo-town" girls, as female students of Achimota are known, can't help but copy the affectations of the boys—and vice-versa. Wesley Girls don't need to.

"Steven, it is a pleasure," Akosua said kindly, rising and extending her hand.

I took her hand. This had gone well; much differently from my dispiriting wait in the office of the Deputy Minister of Trade and Industry. I couldn't thank her enough. Without realizing it, she already gave me something invaluable, restorative, even. She gave me back my confidence.

"One more thing, Steven," she added as I made my way to the door. "I suggest you go see the Deputy Minister of Trade and Industry. This is part of his bailiwick. I can call on your behalf."

Out in the parking lot, I tapped on the window of the Nissan Patrol, waking up Joshua. "Praise Jesus!" he exclaimed, startled from his late afternoon nap.

Da a wo ho nyɛ no, na wo hyia wase.
The day on which you are penniless, you meet your mother-in-law.

*"We find ourselves in our most troublesome
situations unprepared."*

CHAPTER 6

Anyone Else Want to Take a Shot at Us?

Cocoa House was the charming, colonial-era name for the dilapidated seven-story headquarters of the Ghana Cocoa Board, a khaki-tiled building that towered over the most traffic-choked thoroughfare in all of Accra. In the early 1990s, an *obroni* making his way into Cocoa House still counted as a novelty and caused a dozing guard, recumbent on a bench, to rouse himself. He required me to sign a foolscap logbook, while dozens of Ghanaians filed in and out without so much as a pause. My meeting was on the top floor, and the elevator was broken. I wouldn't have taken it in any case. The fear of being trapped in a hot metal box in a country where repairs take hours if not days demanded that I make my way up the crowded staircase, one careful step at a time. I no longer bounded up stairwells in Ghana. Stairways in government buildings of this era are not built to any sort of building code (at least not any code that is enforced), and the steps can be slightly misaligned, each tread a few millimeters higher or lower than the one before. It is treacherous to climb tile stairs absentmindedly, especially in slick-bottomed wing tips.

The Acting Chief Executive of the Ghana Cocoa Board was Flight Lieutenant Joseph Bonsu-Mensah (Rtd.). Though retired from the military, he held the same rank, flight lieutenant, as the Head of State. I wondered why people holding high office here hold relatively modest military rank? Uganda's Idi Amin famously called himself "His Excellency, President for Life, Field Marshal Al Hadji Doctor Idi Amin Dada, VC, DSO, MC, Lord of All the Beasts of the Earth and Fishes of the Seas and Conqueror of the British Empire in Africa in General and Uganda in Particular." Ghana's military office holders were, and remain today, far more modest. Either that or Ghana's military is more of a meritocracy than Uganda's. I'm not sure which.

Everyone called the Acting Chief Executive "Flight," and surprisingly, I found myself addressing him that way, too. Flight was clearly my senior in age, experience, title, and rank. Titles speak volumes here. Flight had served in "Acting" status for several years now, and you might expect that the "Acting" would have been dropped from his title long ago. Why hadn't it? As close to the Head of State as Flight must have been to have received this post in the first place, his "Acting" status was indicative of the way Flight Lieutenant Jerry John Rawlings ruled. Nobody should get *too* comfortable in office. Rawlings had staged two coups, after all. Following the first, in 1979, he handed over authority to a civilian government before disenchantment with its progress prompted him to take over the government again in 1981. This time he mercilessly cleaned house, removing what he saw as a corpulent and increasingly corrupt government. Rawlings had promised to hold constitutional elections, a promise he fulfilled in 1992, whereupon he won two full terms as a democratically elected president. At the end of his second term in office, in accordance with Ghana's new constitutional term limit, Rawlings retired from elected political life, a gesture that caught many skeptics by surprise, for it was practically unprecedented on the African continent. It was a move certain to place Jerry Rawlings in the first tier of Ghana's leaders decades from now, as the man who returned constitutional democracy to Ghana, notwithstanding that it took him two coups and some brutish tactics to accomplish this feat. Those who have not lived the journey take for granted how challenging it is to establish something as elusive—and fragile—as good government.

But in early 1992, both Ghana and the Ghana Cocoa Board were run by soldiers. I should not have been surprised that Flight agreed to meet with me. This administration was not given to wasting time on bureaucratic protocols. As they saw it, they needed to right the ship of state and return Ghana to democracy, if such a thing would take hold. Ghana might be the perfect terroir for growing cocoa, but democracy was likewise a delicate crop, susceptible to infestations and blights.

"Steven," Flight said, "your proposal is most interesting. And it is something we have thought about for a long time." I was encouraged, until he posed a confounding question: "The beans. From where will you . . . *acquire* your cocoa beans?"

Was this some sort of trick question? I looked out his window, ready to make a grand gesture, hoping the lush panorama of a cocoa plantation will magically appear, and with it, deliverance from his inexplicable question. Instead, I saw only spires of smoke rising lackadaisically from a thousand braziers and a kaleidoscope of rooftops all ajumble. No cocoa farms—not in Accra; the farms lie a province north.

Flight repeated his question in all earnestness. Like most Ghanaians, he pronounced "co-CO" with a hard emphasis on the second syllable, before trailing off into an almost sexual moan, "co-COooo."

"Where will I *get cocoa*?" I was completely befuddled. Some sort of euphemism, perhaps? "I beg of you. You grow half a million metric tons of cocoa *every year*. What do you mean, 'Where will I get cocoa?' Right outside this window! Right here, in Ghana! You are the largest grower of cocoa beans in the world, right?"

"This year we are in second place, I'm afraid."

I knew this fact, but didn't want to offend.

"Surely you have tons of cocoa beans, and I thought you'd want to turn some of them into chocolate? You have nearly a million cocoa farmers," I exaggerated a bit. More like 750,000.

Had he read my proposal? Had I somehow left out this most obvious of details?

"Steven, yes, of course we have cocoa beans. Many, many cocoa beans." Flight laughed easily. I felt like a small boy. "But you must buy them from us, from Cocoa Board, from government. We have the monopoly on purchasing *all* the beans grown in Ghana and selling *all* the cocoa beans grown in Ghana. You can't just come here and buy cocoa from our farmers." He smiled kindly, steepling his hands. "Steven, if you want to make chocolate here, we will be your partner, ah-haaa . . . so you understand? You see?"

I was beginning to. I was welcome to build a chocolate factory in Ghana, but as for securing raw cocoa beans to push into the front end of the facility—that was a different story. Unless, of course, I agreed to work with the government. This probably explained why no one else had tried to build a chocolate factory in Ghana. Why would anyone invest in a factory here if the single resource you most needed, the resource that constituted Ghana's competitive advantage—cocoa—was held by a monopolist who was under no obligation to sell to you? What would David Ricardo say? How could Ghana move up the cocoa value chain—from bean to bar—if it did not invest in the assets necessary to build a global brand?

"We have a facility that I'd like you to visit. My colleague Dr. Sarpong is the MD," Flight said, referring to the managing director. "Please see if you both can find a way to work together. I believe this will be the way forward." In short order Flight gave me a letter allowing me access to, and permission to photograph, the country's sole operational cocoa-processing factory, a facility owned entirely by the Ghana Cocoa Board and one that presumably enjoyed access to a portion of the treasure trove of Ghana's cocoa beans not otherwise destined for sales to overseas processors.

Soon, I was on my way to Portem, an aging factory built in Tema by an Italian concern in the 1930s. The structure's most notable feature was a massive, overwhelming cluster of ninety-six concrete silos, towering fifteen stories high, slowly moldering in the heat. They were remnants of an ambitious scheme hatched by Kwame Nkrumah to store Ghana's cocoa beans and thus artificially starve the international market, producing a short-term shortage that would raise the world price for cocoa beans to the benefit of Ghana's cocoa farmers. Nkrumah failed adequately to account for the fact that cocoa beans rot quickly when stored in humid climes, and the silos were quickly and quietly abandoned; they stand today as a legacy to grand vision and unintended consequence—which, it occurs to me, might be a fitting motto for much of the continent's economic history—if not the world's—during the 1960s and beyond.

The Portem factory was state-owned and engaged almost entirely in first-stage cocoa processing: roasting cocoa beans and pressing them into cocoa butter, cocoa liquor, and cocoa cake. These three items are industrial inputs used in both the confectionery and the cosmetics industries. Cake, butter, and liquor are unfamiliar to most consumers, so the marketing focus of Portem was business-to-business rather than business-to-consumer. The manufacture of chocolate had never been a priority at Portem; it accounted for something like 5 percent of total revenues, all of it derived from the domestic market. While the factory did some value-added processing, it did not focus on the uppermost tier of the cocoa value chain—the crafting of fine chocolate packaged for consumers in Europe, Asia, and the United States. And though the factory had just completed a renovation, the renovation was centered primarily on upgrading this first-stage processing equipment rather than the confectionery line.

My first visit, and every subsequent one, began with a formal meeting in the boardroom with the senior staff, led by Dr. Paul

Sarpong, Portem's managing director. Sarpong would offer me the customary glass of water and a warm welcome. A Pentecostal elder, he'd often begin with a prayer, his eyes tightly shut, half a dozen of his direct reports dutifully bowing their heads. By formal training a process engineer, Sarpong was a linear thinker, a literalist, and a man of deep faith who fancied himself sent by God to run this factory on behalf of the state. He also suffered, I think, from severe vocal cord scarring, an affliction that made him sound like Louis Armstrong. I understood maybe 65 percent of Sarpong's rasping.

In time, I sensed that Sarpong perhaps viewed my plan to sell chocolate abroad as an indictment of his factory's inability to secure export sales for their own domestic chocolate bars, branded as Golden Tree. These local chocolate bars were a rough-tasting concoction. I patiently tried to describe how I had developed recipes specifically tailored to offshore markets such as the United States and was paying a small fortune to develop proper packaging for our bars, crucial if we planned on enticing some first-adapter consumer in San Francisco, New York, or Milwaukee to try a luxury food product manufactured in Ghana—a place, I assured them, that few Americans could find on a map.

"I beg of you," I implored, using this peculiarly Ghanaian construction of speech, "no one in the US knows that Ghana grows the finest cocoa in the world."

This was met with astonishment. Every schoolboy and schoolgirl in Ghana knows that Ghana grows the best cocoa on earth. I assured Sarpong and his team that this was not common knowledge in the United States. If I had not lived in Sunyani myself, then I, too, would be ignorant of Ghana's cocoa legacy. I did not mean to insult them, only to explain that *we*—all of us together—faced a formidable marketing challenge. We had to convince people abroad that Ghana could indeed manufacture a luxury food product worthy of competing with the finest offerings of Switzerland, Belgium, and

France. We had to rebut long-held US misperceptions about Africa, a task that would prove far more difficult than the actual production of chocolate in this inhospitable climate.

My marketing analysis was not what the Golden Tree team wanted to hear, *at-TALL. Not at-TALL*. Why couldn't I just place a large export order for their Golden Tree chocolate bars and be done with it? They assured me that they had sold Golden Tree abroad. I later learned that they had indeed *once* sold a shipment of Golden Tree bars to Libya, a personal favor extended some years ago to coup leader Jerry Rawlings from Muammar Gaddafi. Hardly an arm's-length sale.

"I don't believe anyone in the US wants to buy your Golden Tree chocolate. You are free to try. But, in my view, the Golden Tree recipe is not tailored to the US market." *How to say this delicately? As a first principle, we Americans like our chocolate edible!*

"Not only do we need to develop a new recipe, we need to alter the manufacturing process a little—lengthen the conching time, for example—but we also need a new brand name and new packaging. This is what I'm here to do. This is my job, my contribution. We can do this together." I paused, warming to the task. Looking around the conference room table, I beheld seven faces, each regarding me with its own version of disbelief. What a complete waste of their time. *Who is this* obroni? *How in heaven's name did he talk his way in here?!*

The meeting ended quickly. They refused to let me tour the facility and take pictures despite a written letter signed by Flight.

I left despondent.

I returned to Tema several more times, an exercise that was one part determination and one part humiliation. It was also expensive. My father helped pay for my airline ticket for my first trip back to Ghana in 1992, but I had been dipping into our savings ever since. Progress? Some, but not nearly enough. I could not afford any more trips to Ghana, nor could I afford to keep paying for package designs.

I could not bear the guilt of trying to justify to myself and to my wife Linda why this was taking so long. I needed quickly to secure some sort of endorsement from the Ghana Cocoa Board or admit failure and get on with my life.

I took stock of how much I'd achieved. It wasn't a lot. Sure, I had found my way around the myriad of ministries and had assembled an exaltation of deputy ministers and staffers enamored of the idea of introducing a Ghanaian chocolate bar to the world's most demanding consumer markets. But even at this point, over three years since I'd first written to Ghana's Embassy in New York, no one had offered any concrete help—and for me, concrete help meant money. Any entrepreneur will tell you that banks rarely lend to new ventures unless they obtain a personal guarantee and securitization that comfortably exceeds the value of the loan. I thought that the Ghana Cocoa Board, with its nearly $2 billion in annual cocoa revenues, was the most likely source of funds. What's more, I thought, the Ghana Cocoa Board shared a long-term interest in value creation—and I assumed that building a global chocolate brand would take years, regardless of how well-funded we might be.

In my most despairing moments, I wanted to grab the entire Ghana Cocoa Board by its collective shoulders and plead, "As much as I love Ghana, it is not *my* country. It is yours. This marvelous cocoa legacy is not *my* legacy. It is yours. If this whole experiment fails, I can go back home to Wisconsin and become a tax lawyer again. You . . . cannot."

So often it seemed that I was doing all the intellectual heavy lifting when it came to Ghana's cocoa sector. Ghana had an entire Ministry devoted to cocoa, yet I could see no innovation. Ghana sat too comfortably at the bottom of the cocoa value chain, its national wealth disproportionately tied to the world price of cocoa—a price that was entirely beyond Ghana's control—a price set by multinational corporations that had no intention of allowing Ghana to move up the value chain. Offshore buyers continually funded cocoa-growing initiatives in other tropical countries, pre-cisely because they didn't want to be forever reliant on Ghanaian cocoa. Inevitably, Ghana would lose market share. Why couldn't the government take just *one-half of 1 percent* of its $2 billion in revenues and invest in some sort of downstream processing? Making chocolate—whether with Omanhene or with another company—was simply a risk-allocation strategy, an exercise in prudent asset diversification.

Yet I couldn't let my own sanctimony go unchecked. *How dare I pass judgment on Ghana?* Where was I—where was the United States—when the British played one ethnic group against another, fomenting domestic jealousy in order to maintain colonial power? Where was the United States when the human capital of Ghana was shipped abroad in chains, and its mineral and agricultural wealth extracted for meager recompense? My country had not tried even once to add some small value locally to Ghana's gold, its diamonds, its timber, its cocoa. *You don't get to have it both ways, my friend. Shame, shame on you!*

* * *

With the help of Daniel Gyimah, Cogs, and Kojo Bamford, I was kissing a great many frogs. *I* could see progress, but for most every-one else, they'd squint hard at my record and shake their heads. A venture capitalist would have fired me months ago. I could hardly justify another trip if I did not at least get some confirmation that we were ready to produce my recipe.

I shunted between Flight's office and the factory, trying to find a way forward.

Dr. Sarpong seemed to grow more religious with every meeting. Some days, in frustration, I thought that I'd be better off if he'd just give way to his Pentecostal inclinations and speak in tongues. Our meetings at Portem certainly *looked* businesslike. We gathered in the sweltering boardroom around a long table, always with at least five or six of Dr. Sarpong's staff in attendance.

"Where is the price report? Ei!" Dr. Sarpong looked at his Deputy Director for Finance and Administration.

"I shall go and come, sir. I must ask the accounting clerk."

"I am waiting-o. Tsk, tsk."

The deputy returned looking crestfallen.

"Where is it?"

"Aha . . . It is not here. I believe it is . . . umm . . . I think perhaps it is with Mr. Sampson. He is on leave this week, you remember, for his mum's funeral. I think you had granted him permissi—"

"Ei! How many times? Eh? *How many times*? This is no game," Sarpong chastised. I could see that he had no desire to lose face in front of this *obroni*. Sarpong was just warming up. "I am not happy. Not happy *at-TALL*, small boy," he snapped, using the most cutting insult one can hurl at a grown man in Ghana.

Over time, I perceived that Sarpong was simply uninterested in product development, marketing, customer relations, and sales. It took me several more meetings to understand why. He was a process engineer, after all. Ninety-five percent of the factory's revenues came from the sale of first-stage products manufactured from cocoa beans. Cocoa butter, cocoa liquor, and cocoa cake are all priced as commodities; the price is set abroad through the inscrutable, invisible hand of international commerce. If Sarpong could produce cocoa butter at one dollar less per ton than the world price in any given year, then customers would beat a path to his door and he wouldn't have to spend one cedi on marketing. On the other hand, if his costs of production were one dollar *over* the current world price per ton, then his former customers—who showed no vendor loyalty at all—would disappear and seek out a lower price for cocoa butter in Brazil, for example. Dr. Sarpong had a tiny, terribly unforgiving profit window; he regarded his marketing department as little more than an order-taking operation, and he saw no reason to cultivate customer relationships or to deliver a high level of customer experience when the only metric that mattered was: Can you meet or beat the current world price?

This is why selling a commodity item is so dispiriting. Your price is set entirely by the market, regardless of your own efforts, skill, or costs of production. Sarpong inhabited a binary existence: his factory operated in an all-or-nothing world. Ask any of his staff about him and they would tell you they stood in awe (and a bit of fear) of Sarpong's ability to win more than he lost in this high-stakes game, year after year. It took me too long to realize that for Sarpong, manufacturing chocolate—and everything associated with the confectionery line—was but an afterthought to the entire operation. Making export-grade chocolate was, to this process engineer, a most unprofitable distraction that pulled focus away from the efficient running of his cocoa-butter and cocoa-liquor factory. In Sarpong's perfect world, he would produce just enough chocolate to satisfy a cozy, protected domestic market and then be done with the exercise. Exporting chocolate to the US was a fanciful notion, and one fraught with cost and risk. Perhaps Sarpong understood this more profoundly than his politically motivated superiors at the Ghana Cocoa Board, who naively thought they might easily and cheaply capture market global market share from European confectioners, some of whom had been in business for nearly one hundred years.

I'm an optimist. I hoped Sarpong would see the value at the top the cocoa value chain. I hoped he would feel a sense of national pride in showing the world that Ghana can do more than just grow cocoa—it can craft premium chocolate, too. I hoped that somewhere inside that clear-eyed, sober, process engineer lay a man of vision. I hoped he would turn out to be a risk-taker. However, I could see that, for his part, Sarpong hoped I would please give up already, take the next flight out of Accra, and leave him alone.

Once the senior staff meetings adjourned, my real work would begin. I would make my way to the office of either the deputy managing director for confectionery or the marketing manager, and I would ask about trial production runs, milling specifications, melting points, tempering, and conching times. The staff seemed far more excited at the possibility of working with me, once the formality of the meeting was over. Getting out from under Sarpong's watchful eye may have improved their moods, too. I sympathized with them.

I had brought with me to Ghana recipes that I'd developed after reading an out-of-print copy of Cook and Meursing's technical text *Chocolate Production and Use*, lent to me by David Rexford, the head pastry chef at the Four Seasons Hotel in Washington, DC. The book was heavy on math and melting points. Punching numbers into my calculator, I would devise recipes that I hoped would showcase the flavor of Ghana beans and yet retain some of the sweetness that Americans loved, an exercise in balancing ingredients and one that required running test batches on commercial equipment. It is one thing to create a bench sample and quite another to ramp up to full scale production runs where industrial machinery would affect the flavor and mouthfeel of the finished chocolate. I needed production workers who were part technicians and part artists who could tweak machinery, conching times, milling fineness, and temperatures to get the proper result.

In the course of a few days in March 1993, we accomplished a great deal at the factory in Tema, and yet I returned to Accra feeling deflated. It was March 5, the day before the annual celebration of Ghana's independence from Great Britain, and I knew that the entire country would now go on an extended holiday. I assumed we would lose all the momentum and focus enjoyed during the previous week.

That night, back at my hotel, I received an unexpected call from K. B. Simpson, a deputy production supervisor assigned to the confectionery division. He asked me to meet with him over the weekend. "Could we continue to work on recipe development? I think you have brought us an amazing idea." It was my first real breakthrough.

I was bereft when, six months later, I learned that Simpson, not yet forty years old, had been killed in a car accident.

Still, the Omanhene Idea had begun to find some purchase among a handful of the employees. After Simpson's death, C. S. Otoo, a junior quality-assurance technician, took up the mantle of championing the Omanhene cause. In time, Otoo would rise to become managing director of the entire factory.

By October 1993, we started running production samples based on a handshake agreement. The early batches were good—but not nearly good enough to compete globally. In April 1994, we signed a formal production agreement to work together. My fifty-page legal document was a complete nonstarter insofar as any government ministry was concerned, but I wanted some legal protections. I took a different tack and tried to align the economic interests of my company with Portem and those of the Ghanaian government's Cocoa Board. The Ghana Cocoa Board owns outright all the cocoa assets in the country, save the farms themselves; these assets include a cocoa research station, perhaps the top cocoa agronomy facility in the world. The government has a monopoly to buy every bean from every farmer, weighing and grading the beans and transporting them to port; another government company markets the cocoa abroad, and so on. The government is a vertical monopolist in the cocoa sector, a tidy scheme to keep foreigners, presumably huge multinational cocoa companies with superior market knowledge, from exploiting Ghana's 750,000 cocoa-farming families. As frustrating as the system can be for an outsider, I admit it achieves a favorable result most of the time, assuring consistently high quality and therefore securing top prices on the global commodity markets.

I wanted to share both the risk of investment and the upside of profits, and I could do that only by linking Omanhene's long-term interests (profits and investments) to those of the Ghana Cocoa Board and Portem. Such an arrangement would be far preferable to arguing annually over the price of cocoa beans. But I was compelled to keep things simple. The litigious reputation of US lawyers had preceded me, and intimidating legal documentation had not helped my cause. Not *at-TALL*. I distilled my fifty-page memorandum of understanding to the essence of the deal—a contract that ran a page and a half.

We signed the agreement in early 1994, nearly four years after I first called Ghana's Embassy in Washington, DC, to broach the subject of producing export-quality chocolate. I had been wandering for four years and feared I might be losing my way. Like so many others here, I was looking for answers. *Perhaps this is the reason Ghana has so many churches.*

* * *

With my signed contract, I drove back to Accra with Joshua. The Nissan Patrol stalled in traffic on the toll road leading out from Tema. Barefoot boys in cutoff pants and filthy T-shirts carried wooden trays of gum and handkerchiefs on their heads, spitting out a stream of chewing tobacco every so often as they made their way down the queue of traffic. Ahead of us, a diesel lorry farted copious clouds of dark smoke every time the driver put the engine in gear. Women with gap-toothed smiles balanced plastic trays of *kenke* on their heads, the warm balls of fermented corn paste wrapped in green palm fronds. We were waiting to pay the toll of ten pesewas, about two US pennies. It hardly seemed worth paying at all, hardly enough to pay the officials who collected this minimal amount. The line of cars and trucks crawled toward the single operable toll booth. There is still no electronic fare collection. As slowly as we were moving, the traffic was even worse on the alternative routes. Why didn't the government charge five cedis (a couple of dollars) instead of ten pesewas? This likely would provide enough money to repair and expand this rut-filled toll road. I was getting tutored in yet another lesson in real-world economics. Many people will gladly pay a premium for better quality and superior service. Maybe not everybody, certainly. But many. The *makola* market women especially value time and gain nothing from sitting here in traffic. And doing things on the cheap is not sustainable—the toll road was crumbling. Time is money. No one was benefitting from sitting in this queue.

Hardly anyone.

A small boy came up with a bucket and a squeegee, and began to wash our windshield, hoping for a few pesewas.

"Ei! What are you doing? Did I ask for this?" Joshua is banging on the windshield, now rolling down his window and sticking his neck outside to better berate the enterprising boy, all of twelve or thirteen years old.

"Hey! I will not pay. I did not ask for this. Ei! Psssssss! Stop that now. Go away! I will come out right now and give you blows. Go away!"

Joshua turned to me. "These small boys. Ei! I just don't know. They are everywhere now. They should be in school. Ohhhhh, it is too bad. I don't approve of this *at-TALL*. Tsk, tsk, tsk."

The boy finished washing the windshield, put his thumb and fingers together, and touched his lips several times imploring us for some "chop money"—money to buy something to eat.

Joshua waved him off violently, regaining his composure as he rolled up the window, face stoically forward. Joshua sighed loudly, embarrassed perhaps that I had seen the wretchedness of life on the tollway or embarrassed possibly at his own inability to control the situation or simply just plain tired of sitting in traffic with me. He reached down gingerly, eyes fixed on the road ahead, slowly turning the radio knob, seeking the spiritual solace of Reverend Ike's Tower of Power ministry, while a choir of lorry engines idled around us.

Progress, I thought. *Well, at least we're not going backward.*

Agorɔ bɛ sɔa, efiri anɔpa.
If the dance will be delightful, it is so from the morningtide.

*"If one will succeed in business,
it becomes apparent in the beginning."*

CHAPTER 7

The Fancy Food Show

Working with chocolate is a frantic race against time. You have a small window, just a few unforgiving minutes, when you can dip a strawberry so that the chocolate adheres perfectly and dries within seconds to a hard, glistening shell. Dip too soon, and the chocolate never properly sets; the cocoa liquor will separate from the cocoa butter, the butter forming diaphanous paisley swirls, like the marbled endpapers of an eighteenth-century book. Wait too long, and the chocolate becomes thick, loses its ability to flow, and becomes an unworkable paste. On the molecular level, there are at least six types of crystals that can potentially form as warm chocolate slowly cools to room temperature, in the process known as tempering. Only one crystal type results in a perfect chocolate coating, with the requisite snap and sheen. In other words, 83 percent of the time—five times out of six—your chocolate is destined to fail, unless you are vigilant with your thermometer and a virtuoso with your spatula. It's *all* about timing. You need patience as you slowly turn and fold your chocolate as it cools, turn and fold, waiting, waiting, waiting . . . before you strike.

I had been patient; perhaps too patient. Money was on my mind. More than usual. The year was 1994, and my twins were now three years old. I'd borrowed against the cash value of a life-insurance policy my grandfather bought for me when I was born—roughly $13,000—to start this *verkakte* Ghanaian chocolate business. And I had poured even more money into the project over the course of the last four years, money that should have gone to a college fund for the twins, a retirement fund for my wife and me, or any number of other rational, adult-minded investments. There is an adage in gambling: "If you can't tell who the mark is at the poker table, it just might be you." The same goes for business. You spend so much effort trying to convince an indifferent world of the ingenuity and value of your idea that you actually begin to believe your own hype. You *must* believe it. And yet, maybe, just maybe, that indifferent world knows a thing or two. Maybe *you are* the mark at the poker table.

Inexplicably, I felt I was making progress. Of course, I was frustrated after spending the previous four years in all those meetings, waiting for approvals, waiting for permissions, and then waiting some more, explaining my case to anyone who might listen. I was running out of patience, and while my wife rarely mentioned it, Linda was, too. We were now in the throes of intensive recipe development, running production samples on the main manufacturing line. Getting closer to be sure, but the fact remained: we had slipped into our fourth year of product development. A firm launch date was nowhere in sight.

The Fancy Food Show, sponsored by the National Association for the Specialty Food Trade (NASFT), is the largest food exhibition in North America, and it fills every pavilion of the sprawling Jacob Javits Convention Center in New York City. I decided this would be the place to debut our chocolate.

The year before, I attended the show to see whether anyone else was manufacturing chocolate at origin, as I intended to do. Not one company made this claim. We could be the first mover. My goal in exhibiting was less about selling my chocolate than it was to capture the notice of the *New York Times*. Then I could build a marketing campaign with some legitimacy; I could almost see the words before me: "Omanhene, as noted in the *New York Times*." And the food writer I most wanted to meet was Florence Fabricant, the doyenne of the *Times*' Food Section.

I added up the costs of attending. The amount quickly exceeded $10,000. What would my money buy? The smallest available ten-by-ten-foot exhibition booth, along with a table for samples and literature, table skirting, one-color signage, hotels, airfare, food, and drayage, the costs of union labor to bring your samples from the loading dock to your booth.

The next Fancy Food Show would run July 10–13, 1994. If I wanted to exhibit, I would have to commit soon to payment of the registration fee. The foliage on my decision-making tree was sparse. On the positive side was the chance to preempt any competitors and to lay claim to being the first to market single-bean chocolate bars manufactured at origin. As for the negatives, I had yet to perfect the Omanhene chocolate recipe. Manufacturing was proving extraordinarily difficult. I had roughly ten weeks before the show opened and, truth be told, I didn't have anything close to a finished chocolate bar to debut. At the Portem factory, Dr. Sarpong (I hadn't yet discerned what his doctorate was for—clearly not punctuality) displayed little interest in meeting deadlines or devoting much attention to perfecting the recipe. I phoned the NASFT looking for—I wasn't sure what. At the very least, I wanted to confirm how late they would allow me to send in my reservation. Ten thousand dollars is a lot of money. I weighed this investment as if it were my twins' very future. In so many ways, it was.

To my surprise, I got a call directly from the president of the NASFT, John Roberts. Add this to the many unexpected, fortuitous examples of goodwill that seemed to fall my way the longer I worked on Omanhene, encouraging me when I most needed a boost. Still, I couldn't help wondering why I could persuade John

Roberts of the ingenuity of our business model, and yet I struggled mightily to gain purchase with anyone in Ghana. What was I doing wrong?

Roberts told me that, if I decided to exhibit, the NASFT would give me a second booth for free in its International Pavilion, since the organization wanted to showcase as many foreign exhibitors as possible, and they had precious few from Africa. Big fish, small pond wins again. The offer was tempting. Recalling my visit to the Fancy Food Show the previous year, I realized I had two challenges. First, I didn't have enough people to staff two booths. I have one wife and one brother; together we comprised the entirety of Omanhene's sales staff in 1994. More importantly, the International Pavilion was the pariah aisle at the previous year's Fancy Food Show, set at the far end of the cavernous Javits Center. It looked like a *souk*, but without the Levantine charm. Booth after booth of exhibitors from the Middle East and the Asian subcontinent sat behind unadorned tables, with unimaginative presentations consisting almost entirely of open jute sacks containing various strains of rice and lentils. Earnest family members—for they all seemed to be family businesses—with two generations of ownership looking expectantly down the aisle, ready to cajole any attendee naive enough to make their way down the naked corridor. The Africa portion of this International Aisle was as far from the Fancy Food Show's high-end real estate as was possible to get.

I was trying to brand Omanhene as an upscale chocolate, and I wanted to be next to the Swiss, Belgian, and French chocolatiers. I wanted to differentiate my product as boldly as possible: we manufacture at origin, and therefore our chocolate is markedly fresher. But for the moment, my concern was not the amount of space I'd get, it was whether I could afford *any space* at all. My voice sounded foreign to me. "John, thank you very much for your consideration, but one booth, in the premium chocolate section, if possible, will be enough."

My AFS host father, Yaw Brobbey (center), with two of his wives. Sunyani, 1978.

The Sunyani house of Yaw Brobbey and my home during the summer of 1978.

My and my Brobbey siblings. I am in the back row, center-right. Sunyani, 1978.

My siblings pounding fufu in the courtyard of the Brobbey home. Sunyani, 1978.

A cocoa tree laden with cocoa pods.

My father, DW, and me, circa 1991, about the time I started
the Omanhene Cocoa Bean Company.

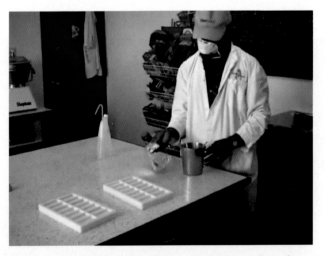

Preparing a bench sample of Omanhene 80-percent cocoa chocolate to get the recipe
correct, prior to committing to a full production run. Tema, Ghana.

Factory production worker in front of console. Tema, Ghana.

Prior to setting up our booth at the 1994 Fancy Food Show
at the Javits Convention Center in New York City.

My father, DW, working the Omanhene booth at a DPQ wine tasting event somewhere in Wisconsin.

Me staffing the Omanhene booth at the Fancy Food Show, New York City.

"Always be selling." Me addressing the African Growth and Opportunity Act Forum at the pink convention center in Accra, Ghana.
Note the boxes of Omanhene chocolate I carefully placed on the lectern.

Omanhene Hot Cocoa Mix stacked on a table at a DPQ wine tasting somewhere in Wisconsin.

Me and the goods: from bean to bar.

Omanhene's flagship gift box of dark milk chocolate.

I hung up the phone, pulled out our checkbook, and handwrote a check to reserve a single ten-by-ten booth.

May Linda and my children forgive me.

* * *

"Five plus two plus one," I said to myself. This was the remorseless math dictating how long it takes to ship a container of chocolate bars: five weeks by sea from Ghana to Algeciras, Spain, and then on to the United States; two weeks to clear customs and undergo possible FDA inspection; and one week to transport the container from the Eastern Seaboard of the US to Milwaukee. Five plus two plus one; eight weeks total. Time was not my friend.

I had purchased an insulated, reusable shipping container the size of a large microwave oven so that we could safely transmit chocolate samples via airfreight. It had four inches of Styrofoam custom-formed to fit inside a heavy-duty plastic shell, with metal corner protectors and custom-built belts and buckles to assure it wouldn't open accidentally. It was crafted like a magician's stage prop; indeed, it made money disappear. The box cost several hundred dollars. The airfreight to send this insulated carton to Ghana and back exceeded the monthly mortgage payment on my house. Until we got the recipe right, we would be sending this box back and forth, back and forth, for however long it took. . . .

Just ten weeks before the Fancy Food Show, the latest chocolate samples arrived via DHL from the factory. I hoped for signs of progress. I double-checked the cover letter stating the ingredients of this trial batch and noting that the samples inexplicably contained vanillin, which had never been specified in my recipe. I never wanted any sort of artificial flavors or ingredients. Further, the factory changed my requested percentage of cocoa liquor by one-tenth of 1 percent. I unwrapped the bar and broke it in two. The chocolate didn't snap as it should; it crumbled. The aroma seemed off. I could smell the vanillin. The taste was unbalanced, the texture poor. I wrote a letter to Mr. Sarpong, explaining that I'd already committed to the printing of 180,000 labels, and the labels do not include vanillin on the FDA-mandated ingredient list because, damn it, my recipe had *never included vanillin*. It wasn't just a matter of ego or taste at this point, it was a matter of law. It is illegal to misrepresent information on a food label. I could go to jail. "Dear Dr. Sarpong," I began.

Half an hour after sending my letter by fax, I receive a frantic phone call from Sarpong. He was agitated, yelling into the phone, and his heavy accent rendered him difficult to understand. The static and poor connection did not help. It was clear, however, that he was angry; he received my letter. I was angry, too.

"*Ei*, what are you doing? Please address all correspondence to 'The Managing Director.' Or 'Sir.' Never use my name. What are you doing this for? Oh, this is *toooo* bad." Sarpong hung up the phone. Bewildered, I realized Sarpong's rhetorical jujitsu had left me metaphorically flat on my back, looking up at the ceiling, with Sarpong's foot on my throat. Sarpong had turned my frustration back on me. He contrived something so he could be mad *at me*. I made a rookie mistake. I am to correspond with the *Office of the Managing Director* rather than the individual who inhabits that office—to assure that there is no whiff of personal favoritism or bribery involved.

All these formalities, so foreign to my US sensibility and my inherent (and apparently inappropriate) lack of pretension, begged the larger question. Why did all these civilities matter? Couldn't you just follow a fucking recipe? How hard could this be? *You stand at the very bottom of the cocoa value chain.* You protect your place at the bottom of the sump pump in the basement of the House of Chocolate as if it were the Golden Stool of the Ashanti. Please, for the love of Ghana, focus on the important things! Or is the proper form of address more important than any technical skill required in chocolate production?

Five plus two plus one.

Eight weeks until the Fancy Food Show opened. A few days after the vanillin episode, I received a new fax from Sarpong, stating that Ghana Customs had impounded our importation of whole-milk powder needed to produce our 48-percent milk chocolate recipe. "There will be delays." Why? Was there a domestic Ghanaian milk industry requiring protective quotas? Had some cabal of hitherto invisible dairy farmers up in Brong-Ahafo conspired to prevent any foreign competition? How much was this going to cost?

Sarpong suddenly became Mr. Communication. Another fax, this time saying he would send the nonvanillin samples, following the Omanhene recipe word for word, as I earlier requested. As if I ever requested anything else.

Five days later, I received two packages from Sarpong. The first was a beat-up corrugated cardboard box held together with cellophane tape. It was not my fancy shipping container, but it contained a set of grainy, melted chocolate samples shipped without any freezer packs or insulated packaging. The bars failed to snap but instead broke apart with rough, uneven edges. The chocolate crunched in my mouth; granules of sugar stuck to my teeth. It was the worst-tasting set of chocolate samples yet received. The second box was my fancy, insulated shipping carton. Perhaps the "good" samples would be inside. Maybe Sarpong wanted to send me every iteration of the production samples. Instead, inside I found only a technical manual for some Nigerian HVAC equipment, nothing more—why the chocolate was not put inside *this* carton, I will never know.

I got up at 3:00 am. It took several tries to punch in Sarpong's phone number, the string of digits seemed to go on forever, and I was sleepy and made mistakes, almost always on the last number or two.

"Mr. Sarpong? Are you there? I think there has been a . . . mistake." I tried to find a word that would sound less accusatory but, *at the end of the day*, as Ghanaians so often say, a mistake was indeed made.

"No, that is not possible. *Ei!* Did you not receive the special box?" This was Sarpong's term for the expensive shipping container. "We always put the chocolate in the special box! . . . What did you say? A manual? What sort of manual?"

"You mistakenly sent me some sort of technical manual; it has electrical schematics. It is for machinery from Nigeria."

"This is not possible."

I regarded the open insulated box, the webbing tangled on the floor and inside, a lone technical manual. Did he think I was making this up? A long pause.

"*Ei*, there has been a mistake. I don't know how this could have happened-o." I hear Sarpong yelling at an underling in Twi, bitter imprecations followed by tsk-tsk-tsk-ing, sighing, and another spirited outpouring of displeasure as if the underling were a schoolboy.

I will never fully understand the Ghanaian penchant for public humiliation of subordinates. To me, it reflects poorly on the leadership skills of those in authority. Did they fail to train their workers properly? Did they fail to give them proper instructions or latitude to make decisions on their own? Why was any failure always due solely to the missteps of some underling? No performance of this street theater would be complete without the bowing and scraping, without the "yes, sir, sorry, sir" shambling as the worker exits, stage left, vowing to do better next time. In contrast to Sarpong's overwrought behavior, I tried to exude calm, but my wavering voice betrayed my frustration.

"Paul," I said, deliberately calling him by his first name, addressing him as my equal, abandoning any pretense of respect based on age. "We *all* fail if these samples aren't correctly manufactured and delivered on time, according to my Omanhene recipe."

"Okay, okay, I shall speak to Mr. Amoaka-Asiedu. He oversees the confectionery line. I shall go and come."

A few minutes later, his perturbation evident, Sarpong agreed to make a new batch and personally double-check the production details. I thumbed through the dog-eared pages of my calendar. There was a Maersk cargo ship sailing from the port of Tema on May 27, 1994. I concluded that this would be the last possible sailing date to get a container of chocolate delivered prior to the Fancy Food Show—and this would require no delays whatsoever. Shipping by sea freight is considerably cheaper than shipping by airfreight. I didn't even want to contemplate the math if we sent even a small portion of our container load by air. The only math that mattered was five plus two plus one, and the math was looking bad.

I had no samples customs-cleared and landed in the US. Far from it. Truth told, I hadn't produced *any* chocolate that approached the taste profile I was seeking: a hybrid dark/milk chocolate, just right for what I thought was the emerging sophistication of the US consumer palate. I designed our recipe to have twice the cocoa liquor required by the FDA so we could label the chocolate as a "dark" chocolate. We'd also include a small portion of full cream milk to soften the inherent bitterness of pure cocoa liquor. In doing so, I wanted to create the world's darkest milk chocolate. I sought a flavor profile attractive to the majority of Americans who grew up eating Hershey bars, but who now wanted something more robust, something more adult.

Ghana is five hours ahead of Milwaukee in late spring. I awoke at three again to call Sarpong. The last batch of chocolate he sent had tasted grainy, which disappointed me because my recipe specified pre-grinding the sugar used to produce the cocoa mass (the precursor to finished chocolate, the cocoa mass comprises the first blending of cocoa liquor, cocoa butter, and sugar). I specified that this pre-grind meet an exact micron size to assure smoothness in the finished bars. Embarrassed by his failures thus far, Sarpong again offered to double-check all the production details, his frustration evident. His voice was more raspy than usual. I'm sure he regarded me as a "small boy."

And yet Sarpong persisted with the Omanhene project. Was Flight ordering him to cooperate? At my insistence, Sarpong faxed me the recipe he'd been using to produce chocolates. I was at a loss to understand why the last batch was so far from my expectations. I expected Sarpong's production recipe to match the confidential recipe I provided him months ago, in which our ingredient quantities are measured in hundredths of a percentage point. Sarpong's recipe didn't match mine. I added up the percentages on *his* recitation of the Omanhene ingredients, and I found they totaled 102 percent, a physical impossibility and a surprising error on the part of Sarpong, the process engineer who often delighted in telling me, "I'm a maths gent." Happily, though, Sarpong confirmed in his fax that *next time* they will mill the sugar to x number of microns, as I had previously specified. That was reassuring, but the fax amounted to a confession on Sarpong's part that he'd been producing samples to a different specification. Whose, I didn't know—but not mine.

Five plus two plus one.

Producing chocolate samples correctly was beside the point if I couldn't get them from Ghana to New York in time for the Fancy Food Show.

* * *

In 1994, communication with Ghana consisted of fax transmissions printed on rolls of Thermo-Fax paper that would fade to an indecipherable smudge inside of a few weeks. Static-laden landline phone calls required me to shout into the receiver, on those infrequent occasions when I could secure an open line. One morning, toward the end of May, I was working out of my house, in an attic room tucked above the garage, the international headquarters of what was no longer Wifely Sprockets but now called the ""Omanhene Cocoa Bean Company."

I had gone downstairs for a minute to do laundry, a never-ending task with twin toddlers. Linda was downtown at work, a forty-five-minute commute from our house; the pressure on her to bill hours was severe, as is typical for a young associate attorney hoping to make partner. My brother, who had come to assist, saw the letter scroll through the fax machine, curling like a tiny Torah. He yelled down the stairwell to the laundry room.

"Steve, you gotta see this fax. It's a copy of the *Commerce Business Daily*." The publication is the official record of all government contracts.

"There's a contract here for . . . hey, can you hear me? Are you sitting down?"

I'm ankle-deep in a pile of Hanna Andersson pajamas and tiny underpants.

"I'm listening." *Do I add bleach to the whites along with the vinegar?*

"There's a government contract to write—get this—a feasibility study on—can you hear me?—a 'Proposal for a Feasibility Study for Chocolate Production Facility in Ghana.' It's TDA Project 93-023."

The implication of this was immediate. My tax dollars, my government, was funding a study to replicate what I had almost fully accomplished and undertaken at great personal financial risk. What's more, my government was funding a road map that could be used by anyone who sought to compete with me.

"Steve, there is only one guy on the planet that is qualified to write this study. And it's you. It pays $285,700."

"Get out!"

"You gotta call the agency that is administering the funds . . . the TDA."

The TDA, or to be precise, the USTDA, stands for the United States Trade and Development Agency. In its own words, it is "an independent US Government agency under the Executive Branch

[that] promotes economic development in developing countries by funding feasibility studies, consultancies, training programs, and other project planning services." In early 1994, this little agency had an annual budget of around $35 million, of which about $1.8 million was spent each year on African projects. In the entirety of the US budget, $1.8 million a year for Africa is not much money at all, a mere rounding error. Funding for Africa had comprised only 14 percent of all USTDA program expenditures during the previous eleven fiscal years. Yet the payoff was substantial. USTDA claims that during the period from fiscal years 1981 to 1992, their funding of feasibility studies resulted in over $400 million of US exports to Africa—an astonishing return on investment. In fiscal year 1994, African projects included proposals for a bonded refrigerated warehouse in Guinea, a coal-fired power plant in Tanzania, a cement project in Yemen and . . . a chocolate production facility in Ghana.

Ask your barista or hair stylist what a feasibility study is, and you get a straightforward answer; it's a study to determine if a project—for example, building a chocolate production facility in Ghana—is possible, is *feasible*. But a feasibility study is not the first study undertaken in the arcane world of the USTDA. There had been a *pre-feasibility study*, termed a Definitional Mission Study or DMS. I paused to consider. I understood the rationale behind a feasibility study—but a *pre-feasibility study*? This was an abstraction based upon an abstraction. A pre-feasibility study invites us to *study*, whether we *should study*, whether it is feasible to build a chocolate factory in Ghana.

The frustration of the last four years boiled over. Why was *my government* spending *my tax money* to study what *I was already doing*? I concluded that I was a shoo-in to win this grant: I was literally *the only person on earth who had tried to produce export-quality chocolate manufactured entirely in Ghana*. Nobody, but nobody, knew more about this tiny bit of knowledge than I. Big fish, extremely small pond.

There were many obstacles to our success: Omanhene was thinly capitalized, my talents had their limits, and I was dealing with a production partner who was far from convinced that this endeavor was worth the effort. But chief among my challenges was not letting myself get distracted. Any entrepreneur or funder of an entrepreneur—to say nothing of my own father—will likely tell you that success has an awful lot to do with staying focused. Concentrate on the things that matter and let slide those things that matter less. *I hear you, DW!* The last thing I needed was to complicate my life by writing a proposal that was due before the Fancy Food Show. On the other hand, $285,700 was a lot of money; winning the contract would buy me time with my most important stakeholder: my wife, Linda.

I resolved to take on the TDA project and to submit a proposal to write the full feasibility study. The due date was June 15, 1994, less than three weeks away and five weeks from the opening day of the Fancy Food Show.

First, I decided to call and then make a trip to visit the head of the USTDA, Todd Kasubiak, who I learned was born in Wisconsin, a fellow Badger. I found a phone number for Todd and called him.

"Mr. Kasubiak, this is your lucky day!"

"Who is this?"

"I'm Steve Wallace, from Wisconsin, and I'm looking at your Project 93-023, the feasibility study for a chocolate production facility in Ghana. I've been working toward this exact goal for four years at my own expense, and I can give you the answer right now for half the price of your feasibility study. The answer is: 'It is feasible.' In fact, not only is it feasible, I've actually done it, and I'd like to invite you to New York in late July, to see how we did it. We're debuting our Ghana chocolate at the Fancy Food Show."

There was a long silence at the other end of the line.

"What part of Wisconsin are you from?"

I neglected to share the fact that we might have a booth with no actual chocolate bars to sample, but eight weeks might yet be enough time to manufacture and ship our first full production run. *Five plus two plus one*, I thought. With luck, we could maybe cut the equation to "five plus one plus one," if we could somehow get a favorable customs and FDA inspection.

I told Todd that his agency wouldn't look very good if it turned out I had already accomplished the very thing his feasibility study set out to review, thereby effectively mooting the need for the grant. What is more, I found a way to produce (okay, *nearly* produce) chocolate in Ghana for a fraction of the cost projections contained in the pre-feasibility study.

So here's how US government foreign aid works: the USTDA doesn't come up with ideas for pre-feasibility studies out of thin air. They work with foreign governments to fund studies that might possibly lead to US exports, thus creating jobs here in the US. It is a near-perfect blending of eleemosynary considerations and self-interest. In this case, the USTDA provided $285,700 to fund a feasibility study on behalf of Ghana's Social Security and National Insurance Trust (SSNIT), the Ghana equivalent to the United States Social Security Trust Fund. In 1994, SSNIT was very likely the largest institutional investor in the entire country; today, it is indeed the largest nonbank financial institution in Ghana, with investment assets of over one billion dollars. And then, as now, SSNIT was looking for places to invest its pile of cash safely, so it would have the resources to pay out pensions in the future as Ghanaian workers reach retirement age. SSNIT, all things being equal, would prefer to invest in Ghanaian domestic projects that served Ghana's national interest, employ Ghanaians, or otherwise build up infrastructure assets within Ghana.

So, the USTDA, knowing full well that SSNIT is one of the few Ghana institutions flush with money, cleverly fronts a few hundred thousand dollars to get SSNIT to consider investing in projects that have a substantial US follow-up component either in terms of consultants, employees, or US-made capital goods. If you are fortunate and talented enough to secure the contract to write the initial pre-fea-sibility study (the DMS), the last sentence of the study has to read: *The case warrants further study.* Then you are perfectly situated to win the follow-up contract for the full feasibility study, which pays considerably more money. If you undertake the DMS pre-feasibil-ity study and conclude the case merits no further study at all, then you are one and done—no further consulting contract for you on that project. You can imagine how few *if any* pre-feasibility DMS reports conclude there is no merit in moving on to the feasibility study stage.

James Galloway wrote the pre-feasibility study on building a chocolate-production facility in Ghana. It is no surprise that he concluded that a full feasibility study was warranted. More astounding to me was his conclusion: that the facility would cost $20 million—$18.75 million dollars of which would be US-man-ufactured capital goods—in other words, 94 percent of the factory would be comprised of US goods. Visit the production floor of any large-scale chocolate manufacturing facility anywhere in the world *including in the US*, and you will be hard-pressed to find 94 percent of the capital goods coming from the US. Chocolate man-ufacturing technology is largely based in Europe, with companies like Buhler (German/Swiss), Netzsch (German), Duyvis Wiener (Dutch), and Carle and Montanari (Italian) crafting the machinery to roast and grind the beans and manufacture the finished choco-late. While the DMS pre-feasibility report seemed purpose-writ-ten to entice the TDA's objective of promoting the purchase of US-made capital goods, the report bore little relationship to an actual working chocolate factory.

While I might have been the most uniquely qualified per-son in the world to write this study, I was not the person best connected to the community of ex-government employees and consultants who funnel work to one another. So far as I could tell, Jim Galloway had never once visited Ghana, nor had he any experience in cocoa processing. Moreover, he had never in his life produced an edible chocolate bar (I guess we shared *that* characteristic).

The TDA awarded the feasibility study to Jim Galloway, and I lost out on the $285,700 consulting fee. In the fullness of time, Galloway would seek out my advice that, in the fullness of time, I would decline to share. I was not going to give away my hard-earned knowledge for free. His TDA report reached the same conclusion that I'd been advocating to the Ghana Cocoa Board: what Ghana needed was a strong partner *with recipe development and marketing skills*; what Ghana needed was Omanhene—or a company like Omanhene.

In the meantime, I had other things to worry about. The Fancy Food Show would open in just five weeks.

Five plus two plus one.

* * *

Another week passed as I waited for Sarpong to complete another sample production run. On June 3, 1994, another Maersk ship sailed from Tema without our chocolate aboard. On a more encouraging note, my preproduction publicity efforts paid off. A small article on Omanhene appeared in *Gourmet* magazine. Two orders resulted— our first customers.

We had no product to ship them.

Sarpong had corrected his erroneous recipe percentages and, in a letter, he reconfirmed the correct formulation. This time all ingredients added up to 100 percent. I acknowledged his corrections and asked for a portion of the order to be shipped by airfreight instead of sea freight, in the fading hope that we would have samples in time for the Fancy Food Show. By this point, we were four weeks from the opening.

The prospects for public failure at the Fancy Food Show mounted. What sort of chocolate company goes to a food exhibition without samples? Yet this would be the best chance I had to garner publicity for our launch. If I wanted to include anyone from the Ghana Cocoa Board, I needed to invite them now. Either they would be part of our triumph, seeing firsthand how much *fun* a product launch can be (and I'm distressed that the potential for *fun*, for joint *accomplishment*, keeps getting forgotten), or else they'll bear witness to Omanhene's humiliation. I wrote to Flt. Lt. Joseph Bonsu-Mensah at the Ghana Cocoa Board and invited him to attend the Fancy Food Show in New York.

On June 17, 1994, Sarpong confirmed by fax that he was starting full production of the Omanhene samples and that he would make the next Maersk, which was to sail on June 24. At Kojo's suggestion, I called in reinforcements.

"Steven, let's ask my sister to supervise," Kojo said. I was grateful for the offer, but I had no idea whether his sister knew anything about chocolate. My mind raced: I trusted Kojo without question, but I couldn't see how his sister, whom I'd never met and who, so far as I knew, had no food-manufacturing experience, could assist. I sensed that Kojo had something up his sleeve. Even over the phone, I could practically see Kojo flashing me a grin. "Steven, my sister Aduah is a food chemist by training. She worked for the US Food and Drug Administration in Washington, DC, before returning to Ghana."

Aduah was more knowledgeable than Kojo and I put together when it came to food technology and production. Somehow, it had never occurred to Kojo to mention this before. Even with Aduah on the case, however, the next Maersk steamship sailed on June 24, without our chocolate.

Five plus two plus one.

I resigned myself to the fact that there was no way we could get a container of chocolate to the US before the Fancy Food Show.

* * *

Three weeks until the Fancy Food Show. Every time the fax chirped, I ran to the machine to watch the paper emerge. Ghana's Ambassadors to the US and to the UN both announced that they wanted to attend the show, as did Flt. Lt. Joseph Bonsu-Mensah. This had become a feeding frenzy! It would be a full-on diplomatic event. Getting wind of the Stateside political interest in Omanhene and sensing, perhaps, that we might possibly succeed, Mr. Sarpong decided to come, too; Daniel Gyimah arranged for him to join us courtesy of a USAID business-exchange program. John Roberts, the Fancy Food Show executive director, graciously offered to give my guests a personal VIP tour of the exhibition floor. Was it possible that things were ripening at long last?

And then I received a fax from Sarpong, confirming that he had sent three hundred chocolate bars via DHL air freight, so in a few days we would have a few, very precious samples for the show. When the bars arrived, somehow I managed to restrain myself, waiting until I could share the chocolate with Linda. She'd been working late at her office, so I phoned her. "It's here, the chocolate is here. I'm on my way downtown." It was around nine o'clock in the evening when she slipped into our minivan, parked in front of her building.

I handed her one bar and took another for myself. I smelled the chocolate through the wrapper, savoring the aroma. Linda had already ripped the label off and split the bar in half. The snap was sharp. Satisfying. The color? Perfect.

I took a bite. I held the morsel on my tongue and pushed it against the roof of my mouth. It slowly began to melt. Sublime! Wonderful mouthfeel. Great flavor. I wondered how we could have gone from the chalky mess of four weeks ago to *this*, in so short a time? But I was determined not to let thoughts of Sarpong spoil this moment. This was a time for celebration.

First, though, I looked at Linda, my toughest critic. My skeptic. She tried the chocolate, thought for a moment, then turned to me.

She smiled as she quoted a line from our favorite movie featuring talking barnyard animals: "That'll do, pig. That'll do."

"I think so, too," I said. "I think we can sell this."

Linda gave me a quick kiss and hurried back to work, pausing to grab another bar of chocolate for her purse. I was ecstatic.

* * *

Ten days later, the morning before the show opened, my brother Jon and I entered the Jacob Javits Convention Center in New York. We held a map of the building; the main hall looked large enough to moor a Navy dirigible. The building was mostly empty, save for random huddles of exhibitors sipping coffee from Styrofoam cups as they contemplated setting about the chore of erecting their displays. The easy bonhomie, that trademark of tradeshow exhibitors, was nowhere to be found. It was too early in the morning, and there was little point in jocularity. Jon and I studied the map, trying to figure out where our booth was located. Duct tape on the floor marked each booth space and the pedestrian aisles, but there was no signage yet. We tried to get our bearings, peering at the floor as if looking for a gravestone. At last, we found our spot.

Next door stood a bearded man in denim cutoffs. He started a company that makes rugelach, the Jewish pastry. He had wheeled in plastic canisters the size of kitchen garbage cans that contained components of a folding booth, which sprang together almost instantly with a tensility that would make Buckminster Fuller proud. Clearly, he had done this before. We walked over to his booth and introduced ourselves, just as a golf cart sped down the aisle and stopped in front of our booth space. The driver's meaty hands enveloped the tiny plastic steering wheel. In the back of the cart, a helper heaved two FedEx boxes toward the center of our booth. The boxes somer-saulted over each other as the driver checked his clipboard.

"Booth 2457: Oman . . . Oma . . . I dunno what the fuck kinda name that is. Two boxes. That's all." I briefly considered telling them both just what the fuck kinda name it is: *Omanhene*, the repository of moral and ethical authority in Ghana and the honorific title of a traditional leader. A paramount chief. But before I could say a word, the driver pushed his foot to the pedal, and the cart sped off.

I felt especially small. Jon and I unpacked the two boxes containing the brochures and a sign I had made back in Milwaukee. I had ordered a folding table, and in no time at all we pieced together what must have been the most modest booth in the entire convention center. By midday, elaborate, pop-up booths with backlit displays surrounded us. Some companies had installed pavilions taking up thirty times the space of Omanhene. I surveyed our simple, skirted table. A banner waited to be hung from the back drapery; once-neat stacks of literature had slid over like fallen soufflés; chocolate bars and tins of cocoa awaited stacking. The Omanhene booth was insignificant compared to the majestic presentation of our competitors. Other exhibitors had employed teams of workers to build the pop-up hospitality suites and to install working kitchens. Jon and I had very little left to do, since our booth was so small and unadorned. I convinced myself that our booth possessed a minimalist beauty. It took some effort.

Jon decided to scope out the competition and returned with his recon: "I just saw the Cadbury booth. It's larger than our house."

"Probably costs four times as much," I said. I fanned out several brochures on the table and stepped back to admire my work. "I think simple is better," I said, still trying to convince myself.

The show opened the next day, and the first retailer to place an order at our booth turned out to be Orange Tree Imports—a specialty food store in Madison, Wisconsin. I had spent $10,000 to come exhibit in New York for an order I could have written simply by driving ninety minutes west of my house.

I left Jon at the booth and went to meet the Ghanaian delegation. I stepped outside the hulking convention center, sheathed in dark glass. Three black Cadillacs pulled up, *always a production*. I suspected that this must be the delegation. Drivers scooted out to open the passenger doors. The first thing I noticed was a pair of magnificent Bruno Magli boots worn by the UN Ambassador. Senior ministers and ambassadors to countries like the US and the UK tend to dress smartly, accustomed to international travel and conscious of the fact they represent, by word, deed, and appearance, the Republic of Ghana.

By contrast, Sarpong emerged last of all, looking jet-lagged; he wore an ill-fitting suit. The cuffs on the pants were so long, they puddled like draperies behind his heels, compelling him to shuffle and slide instead of stepping normally. Back in my Sunyani days, Ghanaian schoolmates resorted to the same sort of shuffling when wearing the traditional red-leather sandals. Sarpong's suit jacket sleeves reached to his fingertips, as if a fifth-grade kid had borrowed a suit from his college-aged brother. With a tight fist, Sarpong gripped the top of a worn fabric grocery bag. Did he bring a bag lunch? Was he trying to embarrass me? Or was he just as unfamiliar with the ways of New York as I once was—still am—in Accra? How much difference was there, after all, between this greenhorn Ghanaian and the American guy who tied a windbreaker around his waist back in 1978?

John Roberts met us curbside, and after a round of introductions, our group set off on the tour. The ambassadors seemed impressed by the size of the venue and the fact that the president of the trade association was here to meet them. I imagined the ambassadors rarely had the chance to attend public events that weren't tightly scripted. They looked delighted to be here. For the first time, I sensed that

Omanhene served as something of a poster child for Ghana. There simply aren't any companies from Ghana with a visible consumer presence in the US. *My company means something.* The wives of the ambassadors accompanied us, each dressed in vivid kente cloth, striking and elegant, with gold cuffs and necklaces bright against their dark skin. Our merry band, wide-eyed at the spectacle of the exhibition, strolled down the aisles of the show, while an NASFT staff photographer, as well as one from the Embassy, crouched to record the moment. I noticed that very few exhibitors were dark-skinned, and our entourage seemed to attract attention. People were respectful, as almost everyone recognized John Roberts, but they did double takes, some outright staring and pointing at our strange parade of colorful African garb, luxury Italian footwear, and ill-fitting suits. I *loved* this. It reminded me of walking the streets of Sunyani, where I would invariably find myself the center of attention.

After the tour, we returned to the booth where Jon was busily engaged with attendees. Sarpong asked if he could set out some samples of cocoa butter, cocoa liquor, and chocolate bars with the Golden Tree label, about as far as you could get from anybody's idea of Fancy Food. He held out the bag to show me. The samples were poorly packaged, with nicked labels and smudged printing—in short, they were a mess, an embarrassment.

"Paul," I say deliberately using his first name—*my town, my pre-rogative*—"I'm sorry, but this is the Omanhene booth. You can't put your samples out here. I paid for this booth, and we are celebrating Omanhene's debut."

Poor Paul looked pathetic.

"I just thought, there is plenty of room," he said, gesturing to the table. True enough, we might have made some room. But that would miss the point. He'd had years to develop a recipe and a brand suitable for export, and he failed to do so. I invested heavily in the effort, and I wanted a minimalist, elegant aesthetic for the

Omanhene booth, one that showcased the simplicity of ingredients and our authentic origins. The Omanhene "look" did not include Sarpong's poorly packaged, paraffin-laced crap that he passed off as chocolate. And, out of rank courtesy, he might have asked ahead of time instead of just showing up with a bag of samples, thinking I wouldn't mind. Asking first would have been, well, the *polite* thing to do.

My emotions were reeling. I needed to walk. I left Jon and the Ghanaians at the booth.

Especially now that I had chocolate samples, I had returned to my overarching goal in attending the show: to obtain a mention in the *New York Times*. I kept a sharp eye out for *Times* food writer Florence Fabricant, though I didn't really know what she looked like aside from publicity headshots. I'd never met her personally. Each time a woman walked past me, I found myself regarding the credential badge hanging, like a long necklace, from a logo-littered lanyard around every neck. But I didn't see Fabricant's name.

Then, two days later, Florence Fabricant stopped by our booth— almost. She stood a foot or so away from the edge of the table, looking, studying, not yet wanting to engage with Jon or me. I confirmed it was she with a quick double take of her press credentials. She had stunning silver hair and perfect posture. I was struck by the difference between her photo on the jacket of her cookbooks and her appearance when working: a reporter's notebook in one hand, pen in the other, and slung over her shoulder an oversize leather bag stuffed with sales sheets and product brochures. I sensed she had had a long day, enduring one enthusiastic business pitch after another. *Please, Florence, one sentence is all I need from you. If not an entire sentence, then a sentence fragment will do.*

She paused, conducting a visual scan of our booth, an exercise that took but a second or two.

I did what I had *been doing* for so many years: I waited.

Patience, patience. I tried not to appear too eager, here in this exhibition hall brimming with unctuous optimism. Then, before she stepped away, I stepped forward. "Thank you for stopping," I said as I handed her my newly printed business card and our brochure. "Omanhene," I coached her: "It rhymes with *cocoa beanie*." She smiled. She was tired, clearly, but she smiled, and her tough, journalistic carapace softened, just a tiny bit.

Victory.

Of a sort. The following day, the *New York Times* local edition contained one sentence—one glorious sentence—about Omanhene, which the *Times* misspelled.

"Omanahene."

Obi nhyɛ kontrofi mma onwe ɔson aba.
One does not force the baboon to eat the tamarind fruit.

*"The tamarind fruit is a favorite of the baboon. There is
no need to force the baboon to eat it. Do not try to teach
someone what he already knows or enjoys."*

CHAPTER 8

We're in Business

With our mention in the *New York Times* and some favorable customer feedback, Omanhene was gaining attention for our chocolate, our business model, and even our packaging. For our flagship box, we received the Package Design Council's Certificate of Design Excellence, an international award. (In November 1994, we went on to win the coveted Gold Medal in the final round of the Package Design Council competition.) *Chocolatier* magazine included Omanhene in its inaugural chocolate-tasting Caribbean cruise. Inquiries abounded, but I had to learn to focus on the sales leads that mattered.

A broker brought us an inquiry from the big-box retailer Costco, interested in a Christmas order of our gift boxes—a $500,000 trial run. But I wondered if we were ready to handle an order of this size. First, our gift box, despite the accolades its design had received, consisted of seven separate pieces of cardstock that had to be hand-folded and assembled, a bit of origami that took several minutes to complete before you could hand-fill the box with chocolate. We would later redesign the box, eliminating two of the components, but for now, either my father, brother, or I was folding and filling every Omanhene gift box. Outsourcing the folding proved incredibly expensive—the many bindery operations I visited remarked that they had never seen such a complicated box. Their pricing reflected this difficulty.

Furthermore, I would have to finance this order—to buy more gift box parts and fund all the costs associated with producing more chocolate inventory—but my ability to borrow any more against my house was nonexistent. I was starved for working capital. Would Costco pay promptly? Might they return unsold units? What was their propensity to claim unwarranted damages or spoilage as a means of delaying or avoiding payment? I had been cultivating many smaller customers to whom I felt a great degree of loyalty. I wanted to make sure I had enough inventory, custom-cleared and sitting in my warehouse here in the US, to supply their reorders promptly. Potentially, it could take three to four months to resupply by the time I accounted for the printing of labels, shipping of the labels to Ghana, undertaking the production run itself, securing a refrigerated container, and then hoping that it would ship in a timely fashion and not be held up at port or subject to a longshoreman's strike or a rent-seeking stevedore or an intensive FDA inspection in the US, or any number of other risks that made it hard to produce within the "just in time" standards touted in all the management magazines I'd ever seen. What were the long-term and short-term consequences if I ran out of inventory for one of my existing, promptly paying customers? Sure, these customers were smaller by far than Costco, but they believed in Omanhene, and you never, ever forget your first customers. To the displeasure of our broker, I passed on Costco with no regrets. None *at-TALL*.

I had no regrets because I understood what we could do well *at this particular moment*. I'd have one chance to make a first impression with Costco, and we were still undergoing our sea trials: working out logistics, setting up office procedures, and redesigning our packaging. Costco would have to wait.

With some other brokers and prospective customers, the wait would be very long. I'll give you an example. I received an overseas call; the phone line crackled with possibility. "Steven? Is this Steven? Of the Ghana chocolate company, yes? I am talking to the president?"

He sounded skeptical. Callers often seemed perplexed to learn that they were talking to the company president. They didn't realize it, of course, but they were also talking to the selfsame person who packed most of the orders, opened the mail, and cleaned the toilet. Today, in this era of automated corporate voice recognition systems, we are left gob-smacked when we reach a living, breathing human being at a company, much less one with a title of authority.

"How can I help you?"

"Yes, Steven, I am Grigori Koropkin from Russia, yes? I have a concern, a big customer, needing cocoa powder. I need you to step up to the plate. What is price?"

Here we go again. It's the law of crazy numbers. It's one of two options: either no one wanted to buy even a single case of my product, or else someone wanted five, forty-foot sea-freight containers a week, starting next Tuesday. *Would it be too much to ask, Lord . . .?*

"Do you want our natural, non-alkalized cocoa powder?" This was my test question for how close these intermediaries are to the actual buyers.

"Yes, fine. Your regular cocoa powder. Standard." Grigori was failing the test.

"So, you don't want *alkalized* cocoa powder—you don't want it Dutched?" I pressed the issue.

"Yes, standard. Dutched."

"Grigori—may I call you Grigori? Most companies sell Dutched cocoa—it's another word for saying it's alkalized. We only sell a non-alkalized cocoa powder, one that's very authentic. We need to confirm what your customer wants—"

"He wants it cheap. It is a big concern."

"Yes, but *I'm concerned* that I'm not your man. There are companies that produce cocoa powder cheaper than Omanhene. We use single-origin beans, and they are more expens—"

"Yes, yes, of course," Grigori said. "But you are up against the Chinese. We must have low price. The Chinese are dealing and wheeling."

"The Chinese are always dealing and wheeling. I'm not your source." I knew full well that these chimerical international customers, with dozens of commission-based brokers trying to source the lowest-price, lowest-quality cocoa, were not our target market. Still, it was amusing, and I learned, anecdotally at least, what the spot market price for generic cocoa powder might be. "Let China have this one, Grigori. We can't win a price war with China."

"I know, I know, Steven. Stick to your shoelaces. But please, China can't deliver until next March." The date that morning was August 3.

"Then China's price is worthless if they can't deliver the product. Tell you what, I'll match China's price for product I don't have, either. Grigori, when does your customer need the product? Can you get me a written delivery schedule? How many containers, starting when, and for how many months?"

"Steven, this a big concern, I already told you. You are losing yourself in details. You are blowing wind in my face."

"How can I plan production without a firm order?"

"Steven, you are more Menshevik than Bolshevik," Grigori said, losing patience, his voice rising in exasperation. "I can't read the mind of a big concern. I don't have crystal balls!"

I considered whether to correct Grigori on his use of metaphor, but he waited for no one.

"Why can't you just give me a price right now?"

"Grigori, we package our cocoa for smaller retailers. I'd have to work up a new price if your customer is truly going to buy full container loads. Otherwise you'll be paying for packaging you don't need. But if you want to place an order today, a ten-pound box of Omanhene non-alkalized, all natural, single-source Ghana cocoa powder sells for $X per pound." I assumed my "small quantity" price was far higher than his big concern wanted to pay.

I could hear the frustration in Grigori's silence. Then he said, "Steven, that is a bad-tasting joke."

* * *

I needed to concentrate on finding domestic customers. Customers who fit our target market: small, independently owned retailers that wouldn't place excessive demands on us. Stores less likely to make us pay for shelf space, known in the retail industry as "slotting fees."

I decided to visit a coffee shop, a local competitor of Starbucks, the sort of place with a strong, loyal following, full of people whom marketers call "first adapters"—customers willing to try something new, who define themselves by the fact they like to buy local, or, put another way, customers who lack a strong affinity for established, national, legacy brands. They tend to be skeptical of big corporations and see right through attempts by food conglomerates to greenwash their niche-product lines. I figured that the Omanhene Idea would appeal to such customers, and, on a more fundamental level, choco-late bars go well with coffee (they're de rigueur in European cafés), and many people drink hot cocoa instead of coffee when they go to coffee shops.

The barista wore a flannel lumberjack shirt over a gray T-shirt. He sported a tattoo of pictographs that prominently encircled his neck in bold, black characters. I was overdressed in a navy business suit. The barista's body art was so prominent, so transfixing that I couldn't help but stare. I was embarrassed by my lack of courtesy. My thoughts raced to the pain he must have endured to get a neck tattoo—and secondarily, how improbable it would be for my stuffy, white-shoe law firm in DC ever to hire someone with such visible body art.

"Impressive tattoo," I said, hoping he hadn't noticed I was staring. "What does it say?"

"It's Chinese," he said. "It means, 'Make good decisions.'"

The barista was true to his tattoo. He agreed to try our chocolate bars and our hot cocoa mix.

There are many ways to bring a product to market, but all involve a lot of legwork if you don't have the budget for a national advertising campaign. Indeed, even if you *have* such a budget, I doubt that national advertising would secure the sort of loyalty and immediacy that face-to-face customer contact provides. I hit the road.

* * *

It was effing cold. Snot-chilling cold. So cold—minus twenty-six degrees below windchill—that I wore boxer shorts over a pair of tight-fitting long johns *under* my wool business suit. This made going to the bathroom a small challenge.

"It's colder than a witch's you know what!" my father said impishly as we unloaded the Toyota minivan, the wind-whipped snow sandblasting our cheeks.

We set about transforming a couple of four-by-six-foot folding tables into an Omanhene chocolate wonderland. I futzed with the table skirt as if draping fabric on a runway model, stepping back periodically to consider the symmetry, before squatting down to adjust the pleats one more time. My father carefully built a pyramid display of chocolate gift boxes and tins of hot cocoa mix. I screwed a canister of fuel into a portable gas hot plate and began heating up two gallons of whole milk for hot cocoa samples. We carefully positioned our two brand-new Cambros, which are large, insulated drink dispensers for the hot chocolate—a steep investment that I hoped would pay off. My father and I tried to make the Ojibwa Conference

Room at the Roadway Inn motel in Oshkosh, Wisconsin, look like Martha Stewart's conservatory during Advent. It was a tall order. I didn't have pinecones, oversized brandy snifters, candles, or the assorted bric-a-brac of Christmas, despite the fact our Toyota Sienna had seemed loaded to the ceiling with craft items scavenged from my basement and, most critically, lots of product to sell.

Jolly Tim O'Toole commanded the room. He used the word "Christmassy" to describe how to lay out a buffet table when entertaining guests, as his chubby digits fastidiously placed a decanter on a floral table runner just so. He enthused about a "big, jammy red" when referring to a favorite merlot. Tim used to perform with the famed Second City improv comedy troupe in Chicago. Today he was playing Oshkosh, with me as his new sidekick, conducting the first of three consecutive wine tastings for a German firm, for which Tim had become the state manager and most successful salesman in the entire country. Under Tim's direction, DPQ (Deutsche Predikant Qualitätzfermenter) Wines sold more wine in Wisconsin than it did in California, New York, and Texas combined. That's a testament either to Wisconsin's capacity for imbibing or Tim's remarkable salesmanship. Both, most likely.

A few weeks earlier, Tim called me, *schmeikeling* for deeply discounted chocolate to pair with his wines. "I'm always looking for something extra to give my customers and thought you might like the extra publicity."

Yes, publicity would be nice . . . but I'd rather have sales. People assume you should be grateful for the chance to give away your chocolate to their school group or book club for free. Do they think that they hold the keys to some undiscovered consumer juggernaut, a demographic segment coveted by corporations around the globe? Well, yes, they do. And they're right. The chance to talk about my product before a community—even if that community doesn't think of itself as a community—is a rare gift when you are starting out in business.

I make it a point never to refuse free product for local charitable endeavors, because I believe it is good for business and, in a karmic sense of justice, it just seems like the right thing to do. Lutheran church raffles, Future Farmers of America fundraisers, Waldorf School parent associations. . . . I love discovering these small communities. They are invariably earnest: devoted to a particular cause and unabashedly supportive of those who support them.

Truth be told, at this moment, I had no advertising budget *at-TALL*. I was desperate for any sort of exposure.

Tim explained that a key part of his marketing plan, his crowning achievement, was the use of hotel events (which he shortened simply to "hotels") in selling wine directly to consumers. He would rent conference rooms in small towns in Wisconsin—places where there is not much to do when the snow falls. He then mailed out invitations offering free samples of wine (a minimum of eight pours of wine), with the caveat that purchases had to be made in half-cases—multiples of six—for any particular wine you purchased. It wasn't unusual, he said, for a couple in Kimberly or Mishicot, for example, to buy $2,500 of wine at one of his "hotels." The genius of Tim's approach was that his customers got to sample the wines before buying. No gazing at intimidating racks of bottles, trying to pick a compelling label or spending too much on a bottle of wine simply because you equated high price with good taste. Tim brought the show to you. Established brands might covet Dubai or Park Avenue, but Tim brought *pallets* of good wine to Oshkosh and Kenosha and Waukesha, with sales commensurate to his peregrinations.

Taking a gamble, I countered Tim's offer. "What if I give you the chocolate for free, but you let me talk about my company, how to pair wines and chocolate—*and* you let me sell my product to your customers at each event?"

"Deal! We get 150 people per tasting, three tastings a day; we start in late October."

Tim thought he had hit the mother lode. *"Free chocolate for a few thousand people? Plus someone to teach my customers about chocolate—and how to pair it with my wines? Product plus teaching equals entertainment!"*

That night in Oshkosh, my father wore a blue apron (I didn't have the budget to embroider the company logo yet), handing out a sample Omanhene 48-percent cocoa content chocolate bar to every person in the room. Tim introduced me. "We're delighted to have with us, as special guests, Steve and David Wallace, the Omanhene boys! And wait until you hear their story and try their chocolate and hot cocoa! He's going to teach you how to taste a chocolate bar so you too can impress your friends when you throw your own swanky holiday parties."

"I'm his brother," my handsome, gray-haired father cracked wise from the floor.

A husband, either hard of hearing or not paying attention, poked his wife, asking her to repeat what my father had just said. The crowd was a combination of middle-aged couples, some groups of younger women—"hunting widows"—whose husbands or boyfriends were out deer hunting or ice fishing this weekend, leaving them to look for some diversion of their own. Whatever the age and whether they were wearing Green Bay Packers sweatshirts, holiday sweaters, woodland camouflage, or blaze-orange hunting gear, the crowd was all smiles. People were here to drink free wine, revel in the holiday season, and have fun. I made my way to the front of the house.

"I'm Steve Wallace, founder of the Omanhene Cocoa Bean Company, and today I'm going to show you how to taste a chocolate bar. Fine chocolate is one of life's pleasures and one of society's permissible vices. Here's how to do justice to exquisite chocolate."

I picked up a bar reverentially.

"The first thing you do is, address the bar. 'Hello, bar!'"

This hackneyed line got a chuckle from the audience, their joviality secured after six pours of Beerenauslese. By this time, many in the audience had perfected the affectations of wine connoisseurs. They also had deduced that it is permissible to ask their wine consultants for additional pours, the better to discern some incremental difference between two varietals. The audience was . . . well, *pliant*. The importance of imposing a two-drink minimum in comedy clubs was not lost on me.

"Now we *really* address the bar. Look at the list of ingredients on the label. You should be able to pronounce everything on the list," I said, launching into a spiel that's pretty much what I presented to you at the start of this book. This time, I added a few lines to call attention to one of my pet peeves. "And, to dispel a widespread myth: while the labels on many milk chocolate bars often show a stainless steel pitcher of cold, frothy milk enticingly being poured into a vat by a fetching milkmaid wearing a dirndl, actual chocolate production does not use milk in liquid form, as it can scald. Look for the use of a full-cream milk powder, instead of skim-milk powder, for maximum flavor."

By now I could practically hear the audience thinking, *"When can we eat the chocolate? It had better be worth it."*

"There should not be a white powder or bloom on the surface of the chocolate. . . . Vanilla, while natural, is sometimes used to enhance flavor, but Omanhene doesn't use vanilla at all. . . . We use all-natural ingredients—no artificial flavors or colors—and a natural recipe. . . . Our chocolate is crafted entirely in Ghana, West Africa, and we were the first company to produce a 'single bean' chocolate bar specifically designed for export markets. And right on the label it says, 'Made in Ghana.' Interestingly, many chocolate bars have names suggesting tropical roots or they tout their single-origin cocoa beans."

Time to throw down the "cheese" card shamelessly. When raising the specter of a rival's inauthenticity, any reference to the East Coast invariably plays well in Wisconsin. "So, while these other chocolate bars might be labeled as 'tropical' or from the 'rain

forest,' check the label carefully and you'll find they're manufactured in New Jersey, for example." Somebody booed. "Not Omanhene. We go from bean to bar all under one roof at our factory *in
Ghana*—just a short distance from the farms where our wonderful
cocoa beans are grown."

These bars had been in a cold minivan for the last two hours.
They were brittle and hard. When I snapped the bar right in front of
the microphone for maximum effect, it snapped, *by God,* like a ruler
being slammed on a school desk. A roomful of people snapped in
unison and murmured approval.

"You know," I said, "I've been accused of taking all the fun out of
eating chocolate." *What?* They wanted to hear my confession. And
it's true that some people think it's a mistake to talk in such detail
about chocolate. I've found that, on the contrary, my audiences want
to learn why marketers promote the percentage of cocoa solids on
their labels instead of disclosing the truly important ratio of cocoa
liquor to cocoa butter. They want to know if the raw cocoa beans are
sun-dried and why. Education sells.

"The best way to sample aromas is to compare several different
chocolate bars at one sampling." At events like this one, I sometimes bring a competitor's bar and pass one around to show that they
don't have any appreciable cocoa aroma at all.

I timed my presentation so that, when I was ready to demonstrate that fine chocolate melts at body temperature, every thumb
and forefinger in the room was marked with a delicious smear of
melted chocolate. A look of relief passed over those who hadn't yet
licked their fingers clean. *We are not slobs,* I implied. *This is what
good chocolate ought to do—at body temperature it ought to melt,
it needs to melt.*

Now the chocolate was melting in the audience's mouths. "After
you swallow," I said, lowering the timbre of my voice, "the taste
is purely subjective. Some may find our chocolate too intense or
maybe too sweet. That's okay. As I say, taste is subjective. But what

you are tasting is pure, all-natural cocoa from Ghana, transformed from bean to bar in a matter of a few short weeks."

Applause! People were oohing and ahhing over the chocolate and comparing tasting notes as if they'd been doing this for years.

I almost forgot to say, "My father and I will be over in the corner with samples of our hot chocolate and plenty of chocolate for sale if you'd like to pair Omanhene treats with some of these great DPQ wines."

Then came the transubstantiation—that miracle of commerce as people rose from their seats and made their way to our little table. People lined up to buy gift boxes of our dark milk chocolate and tins of hot cocoa. The queue of customers ran sixteen people deep by the time I threaded my way from the front of the house to our display. I was so excited, I could barely count out the change as twenty-dollar bills and checks piled up in our battered cash box. *At long last*, I thought, *we're in business*.

It was almost midnight when my father and I broke camp and finished loading the minivan with what was left of our inventory (not much). We stacked the empty Cambros of hot cocoa, drips of congealed chocolate dappling the sides like candle wax. We put the cash box on the floor of the passenger seat. Our voices were hoarse from celebrating the sales we made. Last thing we loaded was our green-metal thermos of hot chocolate to keep us warm and awake. DW and I drove off into the darkness, quiet now, on our journey home, snowflakes aglitter in the beam of our headlights as we passed the dented thermos back and forth across the front seat.

* * *

For a long time, this was how I conducted my oh-so-high-powered, glamorous business. Making deals with overworked baristas solicitous enough to listen to my pitch even as they expertly pulled shots of espresso for a waiting line of customers. Handing out samples.

Driving and flying to make one-on-one connections. Roping in family members to help when they could spare the time. For example, on August 17, 1994, when the first sea-freight container arrived in Milwaukee, my father and I unpacked the Omanhene bars, only to find that nearly half of them had an unsightly scratch across the front of the label, caused by the label wrapping machinery in Ghana. There must have been 100,000 defective labels. I was shaking with anger at whatever employee let the wrapping machine continue to run when it wasn't aligned properly. I found that if I used a damp paper towel, I could scrub the scratch marks off each label. This was a painstaking endeavor, but DW, Jonathan, and I set a quota for ourselves and hand-wiped chocolate bars every evening until we got the job done. I wondered whether Milton Hershey started thus.

To the end, my father was always willing to pitch in and to offer encouragement. We spoke almost every day, usually when I'd call my parents on my commute into work. The last time DW and I spoke, I'd been running Omanhene for seventeen years and found myself in the throes of a difficult decision. DW and Junie Cookie were wintering in Florida and had just gotten back from the beach. I explained my anguish and received the encouragement I needed. I felt bad to have troubled his day with my problems, but by the time we'd talked it out, he had put everything right in my world, as he so often did. Then he laughed and shared *his* problem for the day: "Steverino, I've got sand between my toes!"

Obi pae w'atifi no, na ɔhyɛ wo kɔn mu den.
If someone beats you about the top of your head,
they exercise your neck muscles.

"That which does not kill you, makes you stronger."

CHAPTER 9

Song of Sarpong

Back in Racine, I reveled in the afterglow of the Fancy Food Show. The *Voice of America* radio network called to interview me (the piece was broadcast in ninety-seven countries), and the editor of the *Amsterdam News* called to profile me and the company. Sarpong wrote an uncharacteristically affectionate letter—puzzling me, for he had previously been so formal, so consumed with pretense. Something had changed; he sweetly thanked me for the "care, love, and hospitality" shown him during his stay in New York.

I also had plenty of administrative leftovers from the Fancy Food Show to sift through. Even before the show, Sarpong had begun to question the letter of credit I opened to pay for the container. My bank assured me of the sufficiency of the letter, which was drafted according to terms specified by Sarpong's own staff. Sarpong maintained that his team could not even find evidence of the letter of credit. Curiously, even weeks later, he still hadn't presented the necessary documentation to satisfy the terms of the letter of credit. This meant his factory still hadn't been paid. When you establish a letter of credit, the buyer (in this case, Omanhene) places in escrow with a bank the full amount of money due under the letter, and specifies the conditions with which the seller (Portem) must comply before the escrow bank disburses the funds. In Omanhene's letter, we asked that an original set of shipping documents be supplied, consisting of various original, signed inspection certificates and recipe-compliance certifications. Sarpong had 120 days to submit the required documentation to the bank, or else the letter of credit would expire and the funds be returned to us; Omanhene would thereafter be under no legal obligation to pay for the chocolate. Sarpong's clock was ticking.

The costs of our first production run had long ago been deducted from Omanhene's checking account; we had to establish the letter of credit in advance of manufacture, in essence prepaying for all of the costs of labor and raw materials, including procurement of the cocoa beans. This "lost" money was a hardship for us. Omanhene was not earning interest on this money while it sat in escrow.

I asked Kojo Bamford for advice. "Let him hang," Kojo said. "Did he submit the documents? No? End of story! Full stop. *Finito*."

In my mind, it wasn't so clear-cut. I was trying to build a partnership with the Ghana Cocoa Board. I wanted to establish trust and good faith. What sort of foundation for future cooperation would I have if I wagged a finger at Sarpong and blamed him for not complying with the terms of the letter of credit? I concluded that I would eventually have to pay what I owed, or else the government-owned factory wouldn't continue to do business with me. If I allowed the letter of credit to expire, then I would have to bear the costs of a replacement wire transfer to pay Omanhene's obligation, plus I would have to contend with the administrative burden of recovering the escrowed funds for an expired letter of credit from a bank in Accra. The last thing I wanted to do was to bone up on the jurisprudence of Ghanaian secured transactions. But Kojo had a point: We all played by a set of rules, and we couldn't unilaterally decide when to waive them. Kojo's argument reflected a bit of private-sector swagger, and I loved him for it. If the Government of Ghana wanted to encourage private direct investment—transitioning away from the legacy of postcolonial state-owned enterprises—it would need to learn how to play by the rules of private enterprise. Asking Sarpong to comply with the standard rules governing letters of credit was not an unduly oppressive burden.

I suspected that Sarpong's failure was also an embarrassment for Kojo—an example of an inexpert Ghanaian trying to compete on a global stage and foundering. Kojo worked so very hard to overcome every tired stereotype of a West African businessperson, that when his compatriots didn't exert equal effort, it set him off.

I had seen this once before. Kojo and I had agreed to meet at my hotel in Accra at 2:00 pm. He said he would call me from the lobby once he arrived. Neither of us knew that the phone system at the hotel had broken. Meanwhile, I waited in my room for the expected call, first worried that Kojo might have been delayed, and then angry that Kojo was so late and had made no effort to leave me a message. I didn't realize that Kojo was waiting in the lobby, making repeated calls, fuming at *my* tardiness while the staff kept insisting I wasn't in the room. After forty-five minutes, I decided, finally, to walk down to the front desk—where Kojo shot me an angry look.

When I explained I never received a call from the front desk, Kojo turned on the clerk, yelling so that every person in the lobby paused. The entire hotel staff studied their shoes, heads downturned, a typical Ghanaian response to a public dressing down. Kojo turned to me and snapped, "Get in the car." I sheepishly followed him out. He took a deep breath, both hands on the steering wheel. He turned to me, shaking his head, more with sorrow than venom, and said, "*This*, this is what's wrong with my country. See what I have to deal with *every single* day?" We never mentioned the episode again.

So it pained me to disregard Kojo's advice. Nevertheless, I decided to waive the conditions attached to the letter of credit; I released the funds. I would have gotten no joy from the pugilistic thrill of sticking it to Sarpong and my Ghanaian counterparts. I had no desire to take advantage of them or the situation. At the same time, I was deflated and didn't fully understand why. Kojo thought I was crazy.

Sarpong was off the hook, whether he knew it or not. My next contact from him wasn't a thank-you note; I didn't expect that. But I was surprised by his request. He wrote asking me to help his daughter register for the SAT college entrance exam, as a precondition to her coming to study in the US. I was happy to help. Maybe *this* small gesture on my part would improve our working relationship. Over time, Sarpong sent three of his four children to college in southeastern Wisconsin. Did this signify some degree of his increasing respect for the collegiality between us?

And then one afternoon Sarpong called to ask for another favor. It was late evening in Ghana, and immediately I knew that something was up: Sarpong was never this considerate of my schedule. He was probably calling from home, too, which meant that this transatlantic call was on his dime (or pesewa), not Portem's. Sarpong was trying hard to sound especially friendly, but I could tell he was worried.

"A shipment I sent to a customer has been impounded by the Milwaukee Sheriff's Department," he said. He paused to read aloud. "They say it is 'suspicion of drug trafficking.' It is too bad!"

That didn't surprise me very much. At the time, Ghana (along with most of West Africa) was considered to be a prime narcotics transshipment point, and all imports from the region were highly suspect. No, the surprise was this "customer." What sort of customer could Sarpong have in Wisconsin? And what was Sarpong selling?

"Please, Steven, if you could go to the sheriff and explain that I am a person of good faith."

"Paul," I said as kindly as I could, "I can't vouchsafe for you. The sheriff doesn't know who I am, any more than he knows who you are. For all he knows or cares, I could be a drug dealer. It wouldn't do any good for me to talk to him."

There was a pause as Sarpong reflected on this. Then he said, "But please, Steven, if you could look over the letter and tell me what to do? You have said that you studied the law."

It was easy enough to say yes, and I admit that I was intrigued. About an hour later—the time it took Sarpong to drive to his office at Portem—my fax machine began to whistle and hum. Scrolling out came the notification that his shipment had been impounded, along with some other documents, seemingly chosen at random: the whole file on his Wisconsin customer and a couple of pages that didn't seem to have anything to do with the case *at-TALL*. For all I knew, pages from a Nigerian technical manual might come through next.

One page caught my eye. It was the letter Sarpong had written to his customer to confirm that he'd sent the shipment: five hundred bars of Golden Tree Dark Milk Chocolates, a carton about the size of a grocery bag. Along with Sarpong's Ghana address, the box would have been more than sufficient to raise suspicions among customs agents and sheriff's deputies.

But *my* suspicions were raised, too. Because, until now, I was manufacturing the only *dark milk* chocolates in Ghana, indeed in all the world. So unprecedented was this dark milk chocolate that I had called the FDA to determine how properly to label our unusually high-cocoa-liquor-content chocolate bars.

Sarpong had stolen not only my chocolate recipe but very likely my chocolate bars coming off the production line. He repackaged them, and tried to sell them in the US. Not only in the US—*in Milwaukee*.

His audacity stunned me. What was he trying to gain? I was his de facto marketing department. I bore all of the costs of production, the marketing, recipe development, and transportation costs. Was he jealous? His factory spent 99 percent of its time and energy doing first-stage cocoa processing. My only concern was making chocolate, and I needed his cocoa liquor and butter to make chocolate. We didn't compete with each other. We *supported* each other.

It wasn't hard to figure out what he'd done. He knew—I'd told him often enough—that no American who bought one Golden Tree bar would ever buy a second one. So Golden Tree conveniently appropriated a new recipe for dark milk chocolate. Only Sarpong hadn't had time to come up with his own recipe: hell, he'd only just started to produce chocolates that followed *my* recipe. And five hundred bars isn't a big batch, so in all likelihood this was a *portion* of a run he'd done for me, an amount he thought I wouldn't miss. But if he was going to use my proprietary recipe, why would he sell it in my own backyard? And use a brand name that was like a signpost on the trail leading directly back to him? If I'd happened to visit his customer's business and seen a bar of Golden Tree, was there any chance I would *not* think Sarpong was behind it? Clueless as he was about branding and marketing, he probably thought that, once he slapped a Golden Tree label on an Omanhene recipe bar, it wasn't mine any longer—and that would be enough to assuage any guilty thoughts he had. The good Christian was sleeping soundly—*Hallelujah!*—until the Milwaukee Sheriff stepped in.

"Unbelievable," Linda said. "And this is a guy you're doing business with?"

"I didn't *hire* him," I replied. "Portem did—the Government of Ghana did—and Portem is my partner. I'm stuck with him."

From the start, I'd feared that somebody in Ghana would start manufacturing chocolate for sales and distribution in the US. To copycat the Omanhene model, you could modify my exclusive recipe only a little, and then you'd be able to make the same claims about freshness and single origins and all the things that made Omanhene more than just great chocolate. I'd done everything I could to prevent that scenario from playing out. But I wouldn't have believed that the perpetrator could be Sarpong himself. Without question, he had contravened the spirit, if not the exact letter, of our production agreement. If not for an accident of fate, I might never have found out.

"Sue the bastard," my brother said. But my legal training wouldn't be good for much in Ghana, where the rule of law is costly to enforce.

"I'll bet he thought he was clever, circumventing your agreement this way," Linda said.

What could I do? Complaining to the Ghana Cocoa Board or any other higher-up, I realized, would merely invite Sarpong to devise an intricately contorted self-justification, which might be accepted. Worse, I risked making *myself* look bad: the foreign *obroni* tattling on a God-fearing son of Ghana. I couldn't fire Sarpong, I couldn't sue him, and I couldn't ignore him. Some kind of response was not only warranted but also necessary, I thought.

I wished I had access to the immense store of Ghanaian folk wisdom. With its intricate web of ethnic and extended family relationships and its pervasive "old boy" and "old girl" boarding school subculture, Ghana was extraordinarily good at rebuking miscreants. Once, back in the 1970s, a council of chiefs reputedly gave coup leader General Ignatius Kutu Acheampong a ceremonial cloth with a design that in the Akan proverbial tradition meant "Wisdom is at an end"—a subtle, public rebuke that spoke more loudly than any direct confrontation. Another time, at another durbar of chiefs, another head of state, who also grabbed power by coup, was portrayed in a pantomime as a person with a wounded arm—symbology that meant a head of state was unfit for office. But I couldn't exactly walk around Portem with my arm in my sling wearing a T-shirt with DR. SARPONG printed on the chest.

One thing was certain: I wasn't going to help Sarpong recover his inventory from the Milwaukee Sheriff's Department. I don't know what became of it. I said to Sarpong, "In the future, why not let Omanhene serve as Portem's official representative in the US? I can take responsibility for clearing customs and storing inventory in our

153

FDA-approved warehouse, and we won't have problems like this anymore. There is no need to skulk around my back." That was the only rebuke at my disposal. Sarpong didn't acknowledge it, but he understood it.

The writer and activist Anne Lamott once said, "Hope is revolutionary patience." I agree. I wouldn't have come this far without hope—a hope that persisted when there was no good reason to continue. Ask me what I learned from my time in Sunyani back in 1978, and I'll tell you I learned patience. Since that first trip to Ghana, it had taken me sixteen years to make export-quality chocolate in Ghana. Say what you will, that's patience. But my patience for Sarpong was wearing thin.

Obi soma wo dupɔn tow a, tow, na tokuro da mu.
If someone tells you to chop down an enormous tree, go fell it,
for it may be a hollow tree.

*"If you are faced with a burdensome task, do not be
discouraged, as it may be easier than you think."*

CHAPTER 10

Judging a Product by Its Package

On December 14, 1994, when we had been selling chocolate for four and a half months, we received a cease and desist letter from a Washington, DC, law firm representing Goldbern, a Swiss chocolate company. Goldbern, I learned, derived tens of millions of dollars in revenue worldwide from sales of chocolate to the airport duty-free market. Goldbern packaged its chocolate in a box designed to look like a bar of gold straight out of a Swiss bank vault or Fort Knox. The letter scared me; I could barely breathe. Though trained as a lawyer, and no stranger to litigation, I never imagined how unsettling it was to be on the other side of the table and receive this sort of correspondence—directed solely at me and my company—from someone determined to put me out of business. If the letter was meant to discomfit me, it worked. I was fully invested in Omanhene, good things were happening, but our sales in eighteen weeks had yet to reach $10,000. I had zero budget for litigation. Omanhene was, in the nomenclature of investment bankers, *thinly capitalized.*

Angry and scared, but mostly scared, I undertook my own legal research and learned that Goldbern had aggressively litigated its trade dress—"the gold bar design"—in many jurisdictions, including the US. My reading of the law suggests that it is unclear whether you can legally protect a generic shape or a color, without something more particular such as your brand or logo stamped on the shape. But this is the stuff of law school final exams—ruminations of an academic, theoretical sort. I needed to make this threat disappear quickly and cheaply.

When I began to think clearly, and the fear subsided just a bit, it occurred to me that it was something of a compliment to have Goldbern threaten Omanhene with a lawsuit. And if Goldbern actually felt threatened by our incipient success, that might be a good omen, an endorsement of our potential. And speaking of potential: Until now, I wouldn't have considered duty-free stores a viable channel of distribution—but now, why not? I had a feeling that, if Yaw Brobbey were in my shoes, he'd go into duty-free stores straightaway. *"That man wants to compete with me? Then we shall truly compete—on both sides!"* A few things puzzled me, though. With no appreciable sales to our credit, how did Goldbern find us? Did our international package design award give Goldbern fits?

I plotted my defensive strategy: the David vs. Goliath gambit had been the heart and soul of my thin, operational playbook since inception of the company, and it fairly described every single negotiation or corporate interaction I had faced. I lacked the resources to defend Omanhene in the traditional legal manner: with a protracted exchange of letters and phone calls, all culminating in a laborious formal negotiation testing the administrative and financial resolve of the parties—each keen to avoid the sinkhole of a full-blown lawsuit. But I realized that, with the law unsettled, Goldbern stood to lose more than Omanhene. They'd never lost an intellectual-property case, so far as I could tell. The facts of previous lawsuits involved competitors who outright stole Goldbern's exact look and box dimensions. In other cases where the defendant inadvertently copied Goldbern's design, Goldbern's aggressive litigation posture always forced a settlement before the case went to verdict, thus ridding the market of Goldbern's competitors. But Omanhene hadn't intentionally "knocked off" their package design; I had never even seen it before. Even so, our name was prominently displayed on a multicolored sleeve that enveloped over half of our gold package, and our name, "Omanhene" was distinct from "Goldbern." It was hard to imagine consumers confusing the two brands. As I reflected on the situation, I wondered if Goldbern really wanted to risk a lawsuit. The lawsuit might end with a verdict instead of a settlement, and that verdict that might go against Goldbern, settling the question, once and for all, of whether a company could use copyright law to protect little more than a shape and color. Litigation is inherently unpredictable. Goldbern might lose at trial. I decided to embrace that possibility.

I called Rachel Lebnikoff, a friend who worked as an in-house intellectual property lawyer at S. C. Johnson, headquartered in Racine, just blocks from my house. S. C. Johnson owns some of the most iconic consumer brands in the world, including Edge shaving cream and Off! insect repellent. Indeed, the designer of the Edge logo was the person I sought to design the Omanhene gift box in the first place. I asked Rachel who S. C. Johnson hired when it wanted to scare the crap out of someone trying to infringe on its copyrights.

Armed with this name, a well-known Chicago litigation boutique, I asked the name partner of the firm to write a one-paragraph reply, on his firm's letterhead, of course, to Goldbern's attorneys—a show of force designed to communicate that Omanhene meant business. Omanhene needed to channel that schoolboy Steve Wallace readjusting his windbreaker on the stairwell of a Swissair DC-10. Only this time I *intended* to show that I was itching for a fight.

My strategy cost less than one hour of the attorney's time—truthfully all we could afford. We let fly a solitary stone from our slingshot.

It struck true.

David defeated Goliath. Or at least David sent Goliath on his way.

A few days later, we received a reply calling off the threat of lawsuit and effectively limning the contours of a safe harbor for Omanhene's use of the gold ingot design—which we use to this day.

* * *

Packaging matters. I've often joked that I'm more of a box salesman than a chocolatier. Consumers are first drawn to a product because the packaging—the label, the trade dress—is attractive. Unless my package design skills are strong, I won't have the chance to find out if my chocolate is any good. The true test of a product is if someone buys it a second time. Then you know they liked both the package *and* the product inside.

As an *obroni* in Ghana, my light skin color is packaging that causes no one to confuse me with the authentic Ghanaian article. In Ghana, I'm an outsider in a more fundamental way.

When it's Yom Kippur in Accra, you wouldn't know it from looking around. There is no Jewish Quarter, no neighborhood where quiet envelops the street as people make their way to shul. No families walking together, young daughters wearing itchy tights, little boys tugging at their clip-on neckties. When I first came to Ghana, I had no idea if there were services anywhere to be found in Ghana—it would be many years before the Lubavitchers would send an emissary to Accra.

In 1978, after my stay in Sunyani, I was brought to Accra for a brief end-of-stay visit and placed with a Muslim family. Shafik Natafgi belonged to Ghana's Lebanese community. He married a

Ghanaian; my host mother, Ethel, later told me that AFS Ghana was both proud and a bit worried at the time of placing "a Jew-man with an Arabic man." (Ethel pronounced "Arabic" with the emphasis on the second syllable: "ah-RAB-ic.") They needn't have worried. The Natafgis welcomed me with an outpouring of love and affection. On my seventeenth birthday, the Natafgis threw me a party, a traditional *mezze*, with platters of Lebanese food, hummus, tabbouleh, kibbe, lamb kebabs, and fried sweetbreads. The best present of all was being surrounded by four sisters. I came from a family with one brother, so the experience was entirely novel: the laughter, the femininity, the nonstop conversation as they quizzed their *obroni* brother late into the night.

I recall one conversation, however, when the conversation veered toward religion. The four Natafgi daughters were extremely curious about my religion. I had not told them I was Jewish, but then, they had never asked. In my mind, religion, especially Judaism, was a subject too freighted with preconceptions and misperceptions, so instead of raising the subject on my terms, I determined to let the girls raise it on theirs. One day, I felt the question looming.

Little Maha was the most curious, as usual.

"So what are you, Steve?"

"Oh, Maha, shhhhh!" Samira said, correcting her sister.

"Don't listen to Maha," Salima added.

"Why, not? I want to know. Are you a Christian?" Maha asked.

"No, I'm not a Christian. I'm Jewish."

Maha blurted out excitedly, "Oh, Steve, you are the ones who killed Christ!"

"Oh, Maha, you mustn't say that," admonished Samira.

"But it's true, isn't it?" Maha persisted.

"No, but it wasn't *Steve* who did it. That was a very long time ago," Samia replied.

"Did you kill Christ? Please, you must tell me," Maha asked, her face full of wonder and expectation. Precocious Maha had flirted with me since the moment I arrived, and it was apparent that this question, *the Jewish question*, was the one the four Natafgi girls had been dying to ask for days. The older girls were simply too polite to ask. Maha's question was borne of youthful curiosity, without any sense of embarrassment. It was no more accusatory than those little schoolchildren in Sunyani poking my astonishingly light skin to watch it blush. Kids just want to be kids.

This Muslim family, themselves a minority within passionately evangelical Ghana, had been taught, most likely in the religiously affiliated private schools they attended, the old canard that "Jews killed Christ." How to reply? My mind raced as I tried to condense, into just one coherent sentence, the fact that it was the Roman government that executed Jesus for his subversive political activities, a version substantiated in the Vatican's 1965 *Nostra aetate* renunciation of Jewish responsibility for the death of Christ, etc. There was so much I could say.

What came out instead was gibberish: "Your sister is right. It was a very long time ago." I realized this was an unsatisfactory answer. Maha was searching for the ingredient statement of my personal label, trying to determine exactly who I was and how I fit into the recipe.

The girls looked at me with puzzled faces. Serious faces. Then, Maha giggled, bouncing with excitement. In an instant, the tension dissipated, and we all dissolved in laughter.

Maha slipped her hand around my fingers and squeezed.

"Ei, I don't care what happened so long ago. You are just my new brother. My new brother Steve!" Maha exclaimed.

* * *

Being Jewish isn't a matter of packaging to me. I don't wear a kippah. But my Jewishness is a listed ingredient on the product label, if you will, of Steve Wallace. My way of looking at the world seems very Jewish in a sort of underdog, Woody Allen tragicomic, fatalistic way: life is overflowing with ambivalence and often finds a way to disappoint—if only slightly—at the very moment when we think we should be happiest. It is our lot to persevere nonetheless. And at the end of 1994, with Omanhene launched and going well, I was about to find out how accurate my world-view could be.

Most entrepreneurs fall too much in love with their business. It is very hard for them—understandably—to entertain the possibility that they *may* have gotten it wrong. They struggle mightily to reconcile the unassailable logic of their value proposition with the myopia afflicting all who question them—or so it would seem. Many entrepreneurs truly believe they are the smartest people in the room. You need this singular confidence and optimism to gain any purchase as you ascend the rock face of a new venture. Myself? I tend toward a Midwestern self-depreciation—or perhaps it's a Jewish self-depreciation—but I wonder if this tack has always been helpful.

I invariably weigh the possibility that I might be wrong, that my assumptions are faulty, and that I've fatally misread the tea leaves. It concerns me that, far from being the smartest guy in the room, I might just be the idiot in the room, or if not the idiot exactly, the least knowledgeable. There is much to be learned from listening to others, if only to confirm the fact that occasionally you might indeed *be* the smartest person in the room. The considered path, the intellectual pause, the quieter approach, are not signs of weakness; nor is acknowledging, with clear-eyed honesty, the shortcomings of your own talents or business model. But you must inflect the trajectory of self-doubt slightly, so it becomes a source of buoyancy and nimbleness rather than the cause of crippling indecision. Optimism—especially in the face of disappointment—is critical to achieving success.

My dream of a chocolate factory in Ghana—one that manufactures fine chocolate starting with raw cocoa beans—suggests a narrative arc fraught with the attributes of Greek tragedy. Not "sleep with your mother and poke your eyes out" tragedy, but an Icarus narrative, a journey marked by development hubris.

Fly too close to the sun, and your chocolate melts.

Deɛ ɔde n'ahwedeɛ no n'ɔwe nase.
The owner of the sugar-cane chews the bottom section
of the stalk (the sweetest part).

"A prized item should be enjoyed by its owner."

CHAPTER 11

Divesting Ghana

Ghana and Omanhene shared much in common: we both needed money. During the formative years of Omanhene, from 1991 through 1992, Ghana was not yet a democracy and was run by the military Head of State, Flight Lieutenant Jerry John Rawlings.

As Ghana's new president, Rawlings had his hands full. Ghana's economy had been devastated by a succession of governments suffering from either kleptocracy, economic naiveté, or a combination of both. Some governments were openly hostile to private enterprise—often jailing anyone who found a way to make a little money, so convinced were they that any successful business was necessarily corrupt. Rawlings had little choice but to seek economic aid from the World Bank. The World Bank lends money provided borrower countries comply with a set of behaviors known as "conditionalities." I don't see any difference (aside from pretention) between "conditionalities" and what most people simply call "conditions." But in the nomenclature of international finance, when you want to borrow money from the World Bank, you must accept conditionalities. Why can't economists use economy of language?

As in other countries, after an extended flirtation with Soviet-style economic planning, many enterprises in Ghana were wholly owned by the government. These companies sported ham-fisted, portmanteau names like Goil (Ghana Oil, an operator of petrol stations), Ghacem (the state cement company), or Wamco I and Wamco II (West African Mills Company, two now defunct state-owned cocoa-processing factories). Our production facility was no different. The state-owned Cocoa Processing Company, Ltd., was colloquially known as "Portem," short for "Port of Tema," the area where the factory is located.

The World Bank regards any state-owned business as inherently inefficient—it's often correct in this belief—and consequently it compels a debtor country to divest itself of these so-called para-statals as a conditionality for receiving tranches of loan money. So the World Bank told Ghana to assemble a list of state-owned enter-prises that would have to be divested in short order—Ghana's con-ditionality for receiving World Bank money. The Government of Ghana, in its heart of hearts, was loath, for reasons patriotic and financial, to sell off state assets, the patrimony of the nation. Imag-ine for a moment, if holders of US debt were to tell the US gov-ernment to sell the Hoover Dam or Cape Canaveral. What's more, these parastatals are often sinecures for those who have rendered all sorts of political favors. In return for party loyalty, you get a seat on a board with a monthly directorship "sitting fee," or perhaps even a post as managing director.

Even before the Fancy Food Show, I heard rumors that Ghana would be compelled to divest itself of state-owned businesses, including Portem. I understood, intellectually, that most state-run companies would benefit by having private investors take charge, inject fresh capital, and install experienced leadership. But in rare cases, state-owned companies might turn an arm's-length profit, and a "one size fits all" divestiture solution might have unexpected con-sequences.

So the dance began: Ghana submitted its conditionalities list to the World Bank, omitting those state-owned companies of greatest interest to government. Noting these curious omissions, the World Bank required Ghana to resubmit the list with the missing companies. At the end of the gavotte, after many back-and-forth exchanges, the state-owned cocoa-processing factory where we produced Omanhene chocolate was included on the final conditionalities list, primed for divestiture.

Ghana's delaying tactics failed to subvert the stern, unforgiving realities of borrowing money from the World Bank. If you want the loan, you must sell your state-owned assets on a quick schedule—often leading to depressed prices. You can't hold onto underperforming state-owned companies in the misguided hope that they might eventually be fully valued by the global market. To be sure, the short-term social consequences of divestiture are often devastating, especially if you are a fifty-two-year-old, low-skilled laborer at a company being divested. But writ large, you can understand the World Bank's remorseless position on divestitures, even if you don't condone it.

In our case, Omanhene brought Portem dollar-denominated sales from exports of value-added Omanhene cocoa products. This, I believe, is exactly what David Ricardo would applaud: Ghana capturing profit from exploiting a global competitive advantage. Portem/Omanhene was that rare instance of a state-owned enterprise poised to reap a benefit from the production of premium export goods. And yet, it is precisely at this moment of ascent that the World Bank—assuming Portem was just another poorly managed, debt-ridden, government-owned mess of a factory—mandated its divestiture.

To comply with the World Bank's conditionalities, Ghana unenthusiastically established a Divestiture Implementation Committee (DIC) to oversee the bidding process for the sale of state-owned enterprises on the conditionalities list. The DIC invited Omanhene to prepare a sealed bid for Portem.

Though Omanhene's annual revenues were miniscule at the time, less than $10,000, I began work on a divestiture proposal with an initial bid price of $6 million. My strategy was entirely defensive: without Portem, I'd be back to building a new factory from the ground up, with no guarantee that I'd get access to Ghana's bean supply. In any case, building a factory would take time and a great deal of money. I didn't want to lose momentum at the very moment we were gaining traction.

I was certain the bidding competition would be fierce. Most of the world's raw cocoa was now processed by just three companies: MacFinn, V.S. Hope & Company, and Roissy-Doucette. I still called them the Big Three, and while they competed fiercely with one another, any industry with so few actors, with this degree of consolidation, looks much like a cartel. Ghana's cocoa-processing facilities were attractive, despite the fact they are state-owned. First, much of Portem boasted new, state-of-the-art, German-made equipment that had been just recently installed; it was not your typical state-owned factory with dilapidated, antiquated equipment. Second, given its state-ownership, Portem came with an implied supply line to Ghana's prized cocoa bean crop—one of the two largest in the world. A bidder could condition its purchase of the factory on a *guaranteed* supply of cocoa beans from the Ghana' Cocoa Board, thus assuring sufficient throughput to run the newly divested factory and then some. No one, after all, would construct a cocoa-processing factory in Ghana without gaining assurances that the Ghana Cocoa Board would sell them local cocoa beans at favorable prices. I myself had been through this conversation before.

Once a bean throughput deal had been negotiated, there would be little to stop a multinational corporation from taking some portion of these prized beans offshore, to their highly efficient European factories for processing. Indeed, a previous offshore joint venture partner in Germany was accused of doing just that, resulting in a scandal the Ghanaian press called "Cocoa-gate." Instead of owning a profit-sharing interest in a local cocoa-processing factory run by an experienced partner, as expected, the Government of Ghana found itself holding worthless shares of a local factory effectively moth-balled by its German partner—a partner that preferred to process most of its Ghanaian beans in Europe, where it didn't have to split the profit with the Government of Ghana. Would divestiture result in a sale to a less-than-transparent offshore majority partner? Would it lead to Cocoa-gate II? Would it lead to the end of Omanhene?

As I saw it, the World Bank's conditionalities compelled Ghana to sell a demonstrably valuable state asset—an operational factory with shiny, new, stainless-steel equipment worth several million dollars—at a steep discount. Plus, the factory represented a bonus lottery ticket—Portem came with the Omanhene upside, a strate-gic partner funding an export-focused product development strategy that was beginning to prove successful. *Now* would not be the time to sell this particular asset. At least not yet.

I decided to take my case right to the top. I asked for a face-to-face meeting in Washington, DC, with Peter Wiggens, who headed the West African Trade, Finance, and Investment division at the World Bank. The World Bank's headquarters are a structure so opulent, so architecturally striking, with glass and aluminum louvres, that I could scarcely believe it was located in the US; instead, some fash-ion-forward European capital came to mind, Paris or Stockholm, perhaps. Courtly, with a soft British accent, Wiggens presided over a bevy of fit, well-dressed young staffers who shunted purposefully between their light-suffused offices. Between the élan of the archi-tecture and the employees, I felt I had mistakenly walked into an international modeling agency.

Wiggens could not have been more gracious as I described my predicament. My explication, unintentionally, sounded like dialogue from the film *Cool Hand Luke*: "What we have here is a classic case of unexpected consequences," I said. "I concede that divestitures of state-owned enterprises are usually beneficial, but in this case, as a private investor in a value-added manufacturing endeavor, I stand to lose a great deal if our Ghanaian partner company is not excused from the conditionalities list. Indeed, Omanhene is undertaking just the sort of forward-thinking, export-driven, hard-currency-centered investments that the World Bank seeks to encourage! What's more, the Government of Ghana has recently undertaken a renovation of part of the manufacturing line, installing new equipment that promises to capture greater manufacturing efficiencies in the very near future. And now, inadvertently, the World Bank stands to frustrate the Omanhene experiment, bringing it to ruin just as we are gaining traction." I couldn't stop myself.

"Listen, we both know what three companies will likely bid for this asset, and we both know that they will pay pennies on the dollar for virtually brand-new equipment. The Big Three just want to do first-stage processing, make cocoa butter or cake, and secure access to a reliable supply of cocoa beans. They have no interest in producing chocolate in Ghana. Who knows if they will continue with the Omanhene experiment? Is this the sort of story you want to tell? The World Bank puts a fledgling Ghanaian chocolate company out of business in a well-meaning but misguided effort to improve Ghana's national economy? Mr. Wiggens, you have an unintended-consequences problem on your hands, and I can't imagine it will play well in the press."

Wiggens paused to reflect, steepling his hands. He recrossed his legs, and winced. "Tea, Steven?"

Rules are rules. Wiggens calmly informed me that it was too late to delist our factory from the World Bank's conditionalities list. The divestiture would go forward. And so, to secure production, I had to put together my own bid to buy a multi-million-dollar cocoa processing facility, just six weeks after I'd produced my first Omanhene chocolate bar. Again, it was a defensive move. I just didn't want anyone else to get their hands on the facility and thereby put an end to Omanhene.

The Government of Ghana made a few more attempts to delay selling state-owned assets as a conditionality of World Bank funding, but talk of factory divestiture resumed on August 19, 1994, and a bid submission date was set for July 10, 1995. Flt. Lt. Bonsu-Mensah gently recommended that I start a new factory with the help of the Ghana Cocoa Board, rather than use their existing Portem factory. This seemed like a waste of existing assets, and in any case, the Ghana Cocoa Board was not willing to invest sufficient money in the venture, so the suggestion was moot. Bonsu-Mensah then suggested an alternative, inventive solution. The Government of Ghana could try to divest only those factory assets related to first-stage cocoa processing (the manufacture of butter, liquor, and cake), which together comprised over 95 percent of the factory's revenue. With the lion's share disposed of, the government would then keep for itself the remaining 5 percent of the factory dedicated solely to chocolate production, thus sparing Omanhene from the hardship imposed by the World Bank divestiture. Flight, bless him, wanted to keep one last poker chip on the table, in the hope that Omanhene's value-added production strategy paid off for the nation.

Bonsu-Mensah's proposed bifurcation of the Portem factory was brilliant, and it would safeguard our momentum. But unless the Government of Ghana *and* the World Bank agreed, I'd still be compelled to put in a bid. And under World Bank divestiture rules, once the divestiture list mandating the sale of state-owned companies is set, it is nearly impossible to change it. The reasons are obvious. If the lists could easily be changed, then every country would renegotiate the sale of prized state-owned assets, and the World Bank's loan conditionalities, intended to improve moribund national economies, would never be enforced. I had no idea where I would find $6 million, but I also had no idea how to protect Omanhene's supply chain, short of submitting a bid. So I added to my job description that of investment banker and turnaround artist, and I got to work crafting a divestiture bid.

On July 10, 1995, I submitted my sealed bid to the DIC's supervising clerk, a sunburned Briton, seconded to the DIC from a trade and cultural organization called the British Council, the cultural affairs arm of the United Kingdom Foreign Affairs Office. Kojo Bamford harbored a suspicion—likely borne of his lingering mistrust of the old colonial power—that the British Council routinely engaged in low-level espionage and propaganda work on behalf of Her Majesty's government. "You can't be serious," I countered. "Surely if the UK wants to spy on Ghana, they bloody well have better ways to go about it, don't you think?"

"Ha! I think they are spies," Kojo insisted. "Harmless perhaps, but spies. And so is the US Information Service," he added, without rancor. "You're *all* in cahoots. I'm surprised you can't see the obvious." He returned to the back page of his newspaper.

Once again, Kojo proved right. Hours after I submitted the proposal, this same Briton sent me word that ZBN, a German company also bidding for Portem, wanted to meet with me. How? Why? There was only one explanation: Omanhene's sealed bid was opened prior to the designated public unveiling and immediately shared with at least one of our bid competitors. So much for the integrity of the World Bank's bidding protocol and those seconded from the British Council.

Wɔ de brɛ brɛ na wɔ de hunu ne brɛ boɔ.
If you dissect the ant with patience, you see its intestines.

*"With patience, determination and skill,
one can accomplish the impossible."*

CHAPTER 12

Opening Bids

On August 1, two days before the scheduled public opening of the Portem divestiture bids, I arrived at the heavily guarded compound of Hanspeter Schieber, located in a leafy, secluded part of Accra. Schieber was the face of ZBN, a closely held, global, family business run by an octogenarian German. ZBN was active in the chemical, agro-processing, and fertilizer sectors—an intimidating product list that, upon reflection, sounded as if ZBN could be the Walmart for terrorists. Schieber's compound, the former Italian ambassador's residence, was surrounded by a high concrete wall, frosted with concertina wire and framed by two guard towers, one at either end of the roof. Private security guards in navy-blue jumpsuits, white military webbing cinching their narrow waists, kept watch from the flat roof of the house, rifles slung over their shoulders. Another guard walked the perimeter with a ferocious-looking German shepherd tightly by his side, straining at the short leash.

If the house bore the appearance of an armed fortress or a Bond villain's lair, Hanspeter Schieber, by contrast, was the picture of calm relaxation. He wore white cotton slacks, sandals, and a loose, open-collared shirt. Schieber oversaw ZBN's successful milling operation in Ghana, and I had heard he enjoyed especially close ties to the Rawlings Government. In fact, Schieber reputedly gave the Head of State an ultralight aircraft for his birthday—the perfect gift for a flight lieutenant.

There was no way Omanhene could compete with this sort of influence peddling (and it would be illegal under the Foreign Corrupt Practices Act for Omanhene even to try). I was dejected—and demoralized by the stink of corruption at every level: first, my bid was evidently leaked to Schieber, and second, the World Bank seemed indifferent to companies like ZBN snuggling up to the Head of State in advance of divestitures. It would be all too easy for ZBN to snap up valued state assets for pennies on the dollar—or should that be pfennigs on the deutschemark?

Schieber ushered me into a capacious living room, all white marble and modern, Italian-leather furniture, floor-to-ceiling glass on one side overlooking an outdoor swimming pool, the water shimmering in the moonlight. Schieber walked over to a bar.

"May I get you some pilsner? I have it flown in fresh every week from Dortmund. In barrels," he said, tipping a schooner under the tap. This was an extravagance. There was plenty of locally brewed, cold beer here in Accra, but to fly in barrels of Germany's finest every week! I felt insignificant in the presence of this muscular Teuton.

His wife joined us. She sported the build of a field hockey player, the better to withstand the rigors of the expatriate life, I thought. She didn't look like she needed the pampered protection of this air-conditioned enclave. She sipped her beer languidly.

"Shall we talk some business?" Schieber began, stating the fact rather than asking the question. His wife rose from the couch and left. "You have been working on this project a long time, no? I have been running ZBN's facility here for five years. This is a tough place to do business."

If Schieber had any flair for the cinematic, this was the moment when he would have cast a nod at the armed guards patrolling the pool area. Schieber was trying to be affable rather than menacing. But the attempt was clumsy, and he couldn't disguise the fact that he was a rapacious Karslruhe cat playing with a cornered, corn-fed field mouse—and a Jewish one at that. I found myself trying to remember which Bond villain was played by Klaus Maria Brandauer—and how Bond got the better of him.

"I know of your bid and suggest you consider withdrawing it," Schieber said.

"I don't think I can," I said. "It's already been submitted."

"Well, I know that. I've seen it," Schieber admitted.

Ever the careful lawyer, I added, "The World Bank has a bidding protocol. Rules are rules."

Schieber changed tack. "Fine, but let me ask: Why do you think you can run this factory here?"

It was a question for which I had no convincing answer. It's true that I'd been producing chocolate for several months, but Schieber had been running ZBN's operation in Ghana for years. Our résumés were not equally matched. Neither were our funds and resources. And that led to another question: If Schieber was so well-connected—to the Head of State, to the Brit who leaked my proposal—why did he even need me to withdraw my bid? Was my proposal a compelling one? Sufficiently strong to win the day? A threat? I contemplated the foam atop my beer, as if the delicate carbonation might augur a way forward.

"This is very good beer, by the way."

He must think I'm an idiot. *Of course, it's good beer. It's from Dortmund, dummkopf!*

"I am serious, Steven. Do you really think you can run this factory here?"

I had a few questions of my own, such as how did he get hold of my bid? What happened to the vaunted World Bank confidentiality protocols? In whose pocket was the Brit? To these questions, I had no answers.

To Schieber's question, I suddenly knew exactly how to reply.

"Running the factory, making the chocolate, is the easy part. Selling the chocolate, that's a *lot* tougher."

Schieber was growing impatient. He got right to the point. "So, will you consider withdrawing your bid?"

I rose, extending my hand. "Thank you for your hospitality. I am not in a position to withdraw the Omanhene bid." I would play my hand to the end.

* * *

Later that evening on Kojo Bamford's veranda, while enjoying a bottle of South African wine and a platter of grilled prawns, I conducted a postmortem of my Schieber meeting. Swirling the wine in his glass, Kojo listened and reflected. "This much is clear: Hanspeter Schieber is a serious badass. And Steven, you don't want to mess with these people, not *at-TALL!*"

* * *

On August 3, 1995, the divestiture bids were officially opened. Omanhene's bid must have been resealed to better comply with the public theater aspect of the spectacle: I imagined the obconic Brit sweating over his desk with a glue gun in one hand and a steam iron in the other, meticulously covering his tracks. Mine might not have been the only bid he resealed: Given the fact that my bid had already been shared with the ZBN group, I had no way of knowing what other bids were leaked. *I'm probably the only person of interest in Ghana who does not already know the rankings*, I thought. The highest bid, $23 million, was submitted by an Italian firm that, like fireworks in Turino, made a big noise but was of no lasting consequence. In the weeks to come, the Italian company failed to produce the required bid bond. With the Italians out of the way,

Schieber's ZBN bid was the next highest. Omanhene's bid ranked fourth. As it happened, none of the top three bids could produce a bid bond acceptable to the Ghanaians, indicative either of the gossamer nature of their bids, or of Ghana's institutional intransigence. I wondered whether the Government of Ghana wasn't resorting to its playbook of delaying tactics—including futzing over the sufficiency of the bid bond—simply to draw out the divestiture process because it had no desire to sell Portem in the first place.

As for me, the divestiture issue alternated between a minor annoyance and the black hole of my universe, a gravitational vortex that consumed inordinate time, attention, and, most of all, enthusiasm. I feared the growth of Omanhene was suffering for it. For months, whenever I recounted the latest developments in this ongoing divestiture saga, Linda would listen patiently and then ask, "How many cases of chocolate did you sell today?"

Four days after the bids were opened, Kojo called me in Wisconsin. "Steven! Your friend is in jail. Ha!" What friend? Who? Kojo relished telling a story. "Your *friend*, Steven . . . Flight *Leff*-tenant Bon-su Men-sah," he said, drawing out each syllable for effect. "Jerry has the man locked up. These are some times here!"

Joseph Bonsu-Mensah was indeed under investigation by Ghana's Committee on Human Rights and Administrative Justice, at the request of Head of State Jerry Rawlings himself. I was beside myself: Bonsu-Mensah was one of my most highly placed government supporters. Bonsu-Mensah's proposal—that the government retain its slender holding in the chocolate production part of Portem—would be far and away the best outcome for Omanhene. What would become of my bid, what becomes of my company, now that Bonsu-Mensah was sidelined?

Kwasi Ahwehwɛ nnya nkɔdɔw Boaboa no,
na ɛhɔ nkɔnsɔn didi.
Before Kwasi Ahwehw built his farm at Boaboa,
the monkeys there had something to eat.

"Used to show a sanctimonious benefactor
that you can survive without his assistance."

CHAPTER 13

Amsterdam Makes
an Offer

In the bone-chilling cold of Wisconsin, the warmth of Accra seemed so far away. That was never more true than when the trill of the fax machine cut through the house at 2:00 am. I'd roll out of bed, trying not to wake Linda, tiptoe past the sleeping twins, and make my way to Omanhene's headquarters, which the family called "the room above the garage," more frigid than the rest of the house because the garage was unheated and uninsulated.

One early morning, the incoming fax demanded that I punch Kojo Bamford's landline phone number immediately. I waited for the canticle of whirrs, clicks, and rings. "Hey, Steve! What took you so long?" I could *hear* Kojo smiling.

"So, what *is* this?" I unfurled the fax, like a scroll of papyrus, and tried to make out the return address: the Johannesburg office of a global investment bank. The author was a banker with a recognizable surname, the Ghanaian equivalent of "Smith" or "Jones."

"This chap Kofi Danquah keeps calling me—must be the fourth or fifth time—and now this letter arrives DHL," Kojo said. I pictured him at his office, cradling the phone receiver under his chin, overlooking the production floor of his family's aluminum-fabrication plant. "Yes, of course, I've told him to contact our attorneys. Many times. This guy is a rascal. He refuses to deal with any American law firm. Full stop!"

"Well, you can give him my number, and he can call me direct."

"He doesn't want to talk to you, either. He only wants to deal with me and Omanhene's Ghana office. He won't say who he represents." I wondered whether Kofi Danquah knew that Omanhene's Ghana business office was Kojo's living room.

"Okay, I'll prepare a response and fax it to you to send to Kofi."

"Hey, Steve, you know these *rascally* banker types, these Wall Street boys! Better watch out!" I grinned; Kojo disdained those Ghanaians who studied abroad and then took jobs with investment banks where they trafficked in flotations, mezzanines, debentures, and sovereign guarantees. In Kojo's view, they were paper-pushers—merging companies one year, only to split off divisions the next—*and* taking hefty fees with every transaction. Precocious, yes, but engaged in nothing more than pedestrian financial engineering and adding no real value *at-TALL*! In Kojo's mind, they trafficked in the ether, doing nothing near as adamantine as making biweekly payroll in Accra.

I prepared a letter welcoming Danquah's interest and asking that all future correspondence be sent to Omanhene's lawyers, the firm where, it so happens, my wife worked as a young associate. Linda had kept her surname, and her relationship to me by marriage would not be obvious. To the outside world, it appeared that Omanhene was a client of one of the largest law firms in the country—and this was technically true. I wondered, as I inserted my letter into the fax machine, what role, if any, prescience played in Linda's desire to keep her surname. Her individualism made it certain that she would never take the name of her spouse even if she had married into the Rockefellers or von Furstenburgs. But meticulous lawyer that she is, did she at some point entertain the possibility that her husband might, someday, land himself in hot water? And by keeping her surname, she could neatly distance herself from any misadventures of mine?

I called Kojo back. He had received my fax and approved. But he had bigger news. He had just called Danquah in Johannesburg and asked him, Ghanaian to Ghanaian, who his client was. "Are you sitting down?"

I was in fact standing in my bathrobe, shivering in the icy room.

"His firm represents MacFinn."

I was too stunned to say anything.

"We are playing with the Big Boys, Steven! Steven, can you hear me?" Static percolated through the line.

MacFinn, with annual revenues of some $67 billion, was the privately held (and therefore secretive) multinational commodity-trading and processing firm—and one of the three largest cocoa processors on the planet, along with its competitors, V.S. Hope & Company and Roissy-Doucette. MacFinn had also voluntarily settled—without admitting guilt—a number of investigations with the SEC regarding improper trading activity and alleged price fixing. At least one voluntary settlement was for $100 million. The company's cocoa operations alone realized one billion dollars annually. Why would MacFinn, with processing operations on several continents, engage a law firm in Johannesburg to contact the Omanhene Cocoa Bean Company?

It turned out that Kees Mesman, the head of MacFinn's global cocoa operations, as well as its European brand, called Broekhuisen Cacao, had engaged Danquah to contact me. After some wary circling between us, at last Danquah invited me to fly to Amsterdam, Mesman's headquarters, for a meeting to discuss the divestiture.

This was intriguing. If the Government of Ghana wanted to simply sell Portem to the highest bidder, it could have done so without any regard for Omanhene. I concluded that someone did not want Omanhene to become a casualty of divestiture. It was complicated, opaque: I didn't know who or why exactly, but two possibilities emerged. First, it was possible that someone actually liked what Omanhene had accomplished, perhaps felt invested in our modest success, or had made Omanhene's survival a conditionality of their own. (*"If you want to buy Portem for pennies on the dollar, then you better show us how Omanhene survives."*) Bonsu-Mensah was out of the picture so I wasn't certain who at the Ghana Cocoa Board or the Castle wanted Omanhene to survive the divestiture.

The second possibility was that the Government of Ghana had no intention of complying with the World Bank's divestiture conditionalities at all—especially when it came to prized cocoa assets. If this was the case, then assuring Omanhene's survival was simply a delaying tactic to stall the inevitable Portem sale, in the hope that no credible bidder would put up with the procedural delays, the Omanhene handcuffs, or the meanderings of the Government of Ghana's negotiating behavior. If the government frustrated *all* the bidders until none remained, then it could say to the World Bank, "I beg of you. We tried to sell our assets, but no one wanted them. So we simply can't comply with your 'conditionalities.'"

I had yet to meet the Ghanaian who would not exult in such a clever outfoxing of arrogant outsiders. Yaw Brobbey would roast an entire herd of goats and invite every man, woman, and child in Brong-Ahafo to the celebration, if he ever pulled off a coup like that.

* * *

Mesman's office cantilevered over a canal on the outskirts of Amsterdam, looking out on Broekhuisen Cacao's flotilla of barges, which shuttled cocoa butter and liquor from one processing facility to the next, all located along the canal. Floor-to-ceiling windows ran on two sides of his corner office, permitting me to digest the vast, impressive view of a vast, impressive company. Devoted to the manufacture of cocoa powder, the factory gleamed with European splendor—glass and stainless-steel fixtures made this look like a cross between a pharmaceutical company and a modern art museum. The production floor was so highly automated that it employed only twelve people; robots blew air into empty fabric "super sacks" prior to filling them with two thousand pounds of cocoa powder in a matter of seconds. Owing to a malfunction in the computer that controlled every facet of production, the factory was eerily quiet today.

I turned my gaze from the barges below to Mesman. He drummed his fingers on his glass-topped desk. Omanhene was trying the patience of Kees Mesman, who was used to getting his way; he worked for a privately held company that didn't brook any sort of joint venture or strategic partnership nonsense. This secretive, hundred-year-old company never had to answer to nonfamily shareholders or please Wall Street analysts. Mesman and MacFinn played for *all* the marbles, *all* the time. He was steaming mad that someone in the Government of Ghana had compelled him to incorporate Omanhene in any Portem asset takeover that his billion-dollar company might contemplate. I was sure he could not believe he was devoting so much time to Kojo, me, and our newly engaged Ghanaian lawyer, Gyamfi Sarbah. Yet we had all come to Amsterdam at his invitation. I conclude that some puppet master at DIC or in the Ghana Cocoa Board persuaded him to try and effect a joint bid with Omanhene—either because Omanhene's business plan was esteemed on its merits or because I represented a potential collaborator who could be relied upon to complicate and thereby delay the divestiture process. The longer Mesman and I continued talking in Amsterdam, the longer Ghana could delay the sale of Portem. Omanhene was the gift that kept on giving.

For Mesman, bidding on Portem was almost certainly a low-cost fishing expedition. Not only did he want to buy nearly new machinery if the price was right, most importantly he also coveted strategic, long-term access to the world's second-largest supply of cocoa beans—for his new Portem factory in Ghana, of course, but also for his factories in Amsterdam and elsewhere around the globe. It was understood that no one would buy a cocoa-processing factory in Ghana or the Ivory Coast unless it came with a guaranteed supply of local cocoa beans. And not only would Big Cocoa negotiate for local beans for their local processing, they'd insist on a clause allowing them to export Ghanaian cocoa beans to their offshore processing facilities, as well. Finally, Big Cocoa would bargain for a discount on their purchases of local beans—say a 10 or 20 percent discount from the world market price. And rising from the negotiating table, Big Cocoa would make their way to the door, pause briefly, turn to their Ghanaian counterparts, and ask for one more thing: a first option to buy the late-season "light crop" beans that traditionally are considered too small for export but can be extremely profitable for domestic processing if the price is adequately discounted. Game, set, match.

I wanted Portem, too. Not because I was in any position to challenge the likes of MacFinn, V.S. Hope & Company, and Roissy-Doucette in the manufacture and sale of cocoa butter or liquor, but because these products are the ingredients needed to produce Omanhene chocolate. For me, the theme song was "Stayin' Alive."

A brutal negotiator, Mesman fell suspiciously silent when I asked how MacFinn and Omanhene might work together in a postdivestiture world. Mesman wanted us to get out of his office and out of his deal. It was all he could do to tolerate the legal fiction that Omanhene would voluntarily withdraw its bid on the condition of working with MacFinn postdivestiture. MacFinn's cocoa operations alone realized over a billion dollars annually. Why would Mesman give a damn about Omanhene?

I suggested, as artfully as I could, ways in which Omanhene and Broekhuisen might prevail in the bidding for Portem by working together. Mesman was having none of it. Finally, in frustration, he pushed a slip of folded paper across the table and said, "Here's what

I'm authorized to give you to withdraw your bid from this deal." Handwritten on the paper was the figure $250,000.

Omanhene's annual revenues at the time were less than $36,000.

I excused myself to confer with Kojo Bamford and Gyamfi. Our "conference" was purely for show; I had read in *The Idiot's Guide to Negotiation* that you never accept the first offer. While I was confident in my ability to analyze the situation from a macro point of view—understanding the relative merits of each side of the argument—I was much less sure about my ability to out-negotiate this Dutchman who was an expert commodity trader.

I allowed ten minutes to elapse—a period appropriate to give the illusion we were involved in deep reflection and intense number-crunching—before returning to Mesman's office. "We've decided to decline your offer," I said, waiting for him to up the ante. But despite his Hanseatic reserve, I could tell Mesman was livid.

"The offer is $250,000," he says. "Take it or leave it."

The *Idiot's Guide* did not prepare me for this. But this partnership could never work. Mesman had no interest in a production partnership with Omanhene going forward. MacFinn's preferred divestiture acquisition strategy, from what I had researched, precluded any minority partners. In any case, I believed Omanhene was worth far more than he offered, despite our annual revenues. Only later did it occur to me why Mesman didn't raise his offer. He didn't raise the amount because he couldn't. He had no authority to increase the offer. For any transaction over $250,000—a fitting round number— perhaps he needed board approval, and he was unwilling to share with his board or superior the messy details necessary to close a deal in Ghana. Mesman bet the house limit on the very first shuffle of the deck. I also concluded that his insistence on using the South African office of his investment bank and his obstinacy in corresponding only with Omanhene's Ghana office—avoiding any direct contact with me or Omanhene USA—might have something to do with his willingness to engage in behavior that might be illegal in the US.

I declined Mesman's offer to withdraw Omanhene's bid, though I left open the possibility that MacFinn could join Omanhene's bid. I had yet to secure a strategic production partner for purposes of the divestiture, but I had one last card to play, one I kept secret from Mesman. Just before leaving for Amsterdam, I made a call to V.S. Hope & Company, a Big Three cocoa processor, and MacFinn's bitter rival.

Ti nyinaa sɛ, na emu asɛm nyɛ pɛ.
All heads may look the same, but the thoughts inside of them
are not the same.

"Conduct and character differ."

CHAPTER 14

Bannerman's Hope

Growing up in Milwaukee, I associated commerce not with the color of money, but with the smell of it. Driving east, toward the lakefront from the old County Stadium, you'd first inhale the musk of the Froedtert malting operation that for decades had served the city's brewing industry. I'd sit with my brother in the back seat of the Pontiac station wagon, holding our breath and pulling faces, as we next passed the Red Star Yeast factory with its decidedly unpleasant odor, made worse on hot summer days. Turning north, toward Green Bay, we'd be rewarded, at long last, by the glorious Ambrosia chocolate factory, with its magnificent aroma rising from what my brother and I imagined were copper vats full of burbling, viscous chocolate.

Ambrosia was sold to the V.S. Hope & Company food conglomerate in 1964. V.S. Hope & Company later closed its downtown Milwaukee plant and in 1992 built a $90 million factory in an industrial park just west of the city. Between the move and the advent of new air-quality emissions regulations, there is no longer the intoxicating aroma of chocolate permeating downtown Milwaukee.

The head of V.S. Hope & Company was Gareth Bannerman, a soft-spoken Englishman who rose to leadership from the manufacturing side of the business. This fact alone made him something of an outsider in a world of corporate leaders increasingly composed of finance or marketing types: people who were deal makers, not chocolate makers. Bannerman was also a champion of youth and a man unimpressed with either pedigree or formality. These character traits help to explain why he retained as his personal accountant a high school classmate of mine, Jeffrey Frank, who worked in a two-person practice with his father. Jeffrey was instrumental in helping me launch Omanhene. Gareth could have hired any white-shoe accountancy firm, but instead he chose a small Milwaukee firm. The first time I learned that I had even a tenuous connection to V.S. Hope & Company or to Bannerman was in 1994, when I confided in Jeffrey my concerns about the divestiture situation and my distaste for doing a deal with MacFinn. Jeffrey offered to set up a meeting with his client, Gareth Bannerman.

Bannerman oversaw the construction of V.S. Hope & Company's new factory in Milwaukee. During an early meeting and tour of this facility, he showed me the trading floor—a diminutive version of the Chicago Mercantile—where Hope's traders bought and sold cocoa futures to supply factories across the globe.

I showed Gareth a few snapshots of our modest factory floor in Ghana.

"You see these rollers?" he asked, pointing to my photo of a five-roller mill, a thin ribbon of ground cocoa running along the center of the platen. "The alignment is wrong. The cocoa mass should be evenly dispersed across the full length of the roller. You are wasting 70, maybe 80, percent of your production capacity."

He flipped through the other half-dozen photos and with each suggested an improvement. I wondered how many CEOs had such a deep knowledge of machinery calibration. My admiration for him swelled.

"Mr. Bannerman," I ventured, "would V.S. Hope & Company have an interest in partnering with Omanhene on a divestiture bid in Ghana?"

Intrigued by the Portem possibility, Bannerman was happy to entertain a place at the table for Omanhene's chocolate operations in a post-divestiture world. Bannerman at least understood and accepted that the table stakes for the divestiture included Omanhene's survivability. "Steven, this is a fascinating company you've built. What an incredible idea! I admire your perseverance. That said," he reflected soberly, "I probably would have fired you long ago. It's just not how we would have done things." But the allure of securing a steady supply of premium beans, plus the chance to add production capacity, proved a strong incentive.

Bannerman arranged a meeting at the New York headquarters of V.S. Hope & Company, and I flew out with the most senior corporate-transaction attorney at my wife's firm. Hope seemed to be everything that MacFinn was not; Hope executives were communicative, and they displayed cultural competence and an interest in operating in Ghana. Above all, they were genuinely enthusiastic about keeping Omanhene in the deal, and they had maintained minority partners before in other acquisitions. I allowed myself to revel briefly in the knowledge that I'd brought two billion-dollar companies to the divestiture bargaining table for the ultimate benefit of the Government of Ghana.

Bannerman was true to his word, delivering a letter of intent from V.S. Hope & Company to partner with Omanhene for purposes of the Portem divestiture.

A few days later, I get a call from Bannerman's secretary. I returned to his office. "I'm terribly sorry, Steven," Bannerman said, "but Hope cannot proceed with this transaction after all. V.S. Hope & Company has just decided to accept a $430 million offer to sell its global cocoa operation to the privately-held commodities giant, Bowman-Lyons-Eastman, known as BLE."

Mintumi mmorɔsa nom a, mɛnom ahai.
If I cannot drink fine rum, then I will drink beer.

"If I cannot accomplish greatness, then I will focus on more modest achievements, according to my capabilities."

CHAPTER 15

Mr. Wallace Goes to Washington

Almost a year after the DIC publically opened the Portem bids, none of the top three bids had been accepted. Suspiciously, all three bidders failed to supply a sufficient bid bond—at least that was the official explanation. Nor had DIC invited Omanhene to enter formal divestiture negotiations, the obvious next step if the top three previous bidders failed to comply with the rules. I weighed my options. The absence of a decision on divestiture was tantamount to a good decision for Omanhene; it meant we could continue production in partnership with Portem, at least in the short term. Maybe this delay-and-see gambit was the Government of Ghana's desired end game: wait for the World Bank to find other conditionalities to pursue so that Portem remained part of the national cocoa patrimony. If Omanhene likewise waited out the divestiture, then we just might prevail and get what we wanted, too. On the other hand, the uncertainty swirling around divestiture dissuaded me (and other potential investors) from funding the Omanhene project. It's arduous to raise funds for growth when, at any moment, your government-mandated production partner might be sold. I understood the patriotic, economic imperative of my beloved Ghana and its unwillingness to sell Portem. But I accepted the inevitability of loan requirements imposed by any creditor. I could not predict who would prevail in this high-stakes game of Chocolate Hold 'em: the World Bank or the Government of Ghana? Who will blink first? *Chicken or fish?*

I decided to press the Government of Ghana to resolve the Portem divestiture. The waiting-game limbo was draining, both emotionally and financially. I turned to the US government for help, hoping they might persuade Ghana to invite Omanhene to negotiate for Portem—or at least persuade Ghana to choose an Omanhene-friendly bidder so that a US company might benefit.

Omanhene couldn't afford Washington lobbyists. Instead, I relied on the inherent appeal of the Omanhene Idea—and any personal connections I could cultivate. These included Ghana's Ambassador to the US, Arthur Antwi, who (as luck would have it) knew President Clinton from his Arkansas days; and Senator Russ Feingold of Wisconsin, who (as luck would also have it) chaired the Senate Foreign Relations Committee's Subcommittee on African Affairs. In February 1996, I learned that Secretary of Commerce Ron Brown was planning a trade mission to West Africa that would include a stop in Ghana, and that, during the trip, bilateral trade negotiations—including trade advocacy—would take place. Secretary Brown's outstanding staff were enthusiastic about the Omanhene story and offered to bring secretarial-level advocacy to bear on the divestiture issue. For the Department of Commerce, it was a question of a US company, Omanhene, facing potential discrimination and unfair dealing at the hands of a foreign government, Ghana, with a shadowy German company benefitting. And all the parties were covered in chocolate. Commerce was itching for this fight. I was too.

Secretary Brown delighted in advocating on behalf US firms doing business abroad and made it a top priority. A relentless traveler who relished *the business* of doing business, Brown understood that US firms are often at a disadvantage when competing internationally. For example, German firms can legally take a tax deduction for what amount to bribes paid to foreign governments. US law forbids companies from offering bribes, a rule that obviously works to the detriment of US firms competing for overseas contracts. Secretary Brown was determined to level this playing field as best he could by using his bully pulpit and his gregarious personality to promote US companies abroad. Learning of Omanhene and our divestiture dilemma, his office framed the situation as one in which a German company, ZBN, might be getting preferential treatment at the expense of Omanhene. In no time at all, a decision was reached to include Omanhene on the agenda of top-level advocacy.

At the last minute, I decided to go to Ghana to participate in that leg of Ron Brown's trade mission. The trip was an unexpected expense, and the timing was difficult, both in maintaining Omanhene's domestic business and on my own home front. I would miss my twins' sixth birthday. I hoped Hannah and Josh would understand. And all the while, I continued to pour into this crazy Ghanaian chocolate business money that should have gone into the children's college fund.

Kojo Bamford and I were invited to attend Secretary Brown's keynote luncheon address in Accra. The Secretary commanded the podium. Goodwill and high expectation filled the ballroom. Brown said that he wanted to highlight "three US companies doing wonderful work here in Ghana." I winked at Kojo, who sat across the table from me. When we were not the first company mentioned, I was still brimming with optimism. Surely the Secretary was saving Omanhene for special recognition. Then he mentioned a second company on the trade mission, also not Omanhene. I surmised: he was saving the best for last. Then he mentioned the third company . . . and it wasn't Omanhene, either. Shattering disappointment! I caught my breath. This is how it feels to force a smile when *your* Oscar's just been awarded to Tom Hanks. Kojo looked at me incredulously as if to say, *"I thought Omanhene was on the agenda, what happened?"*

What was I thinking, anyway? The companies mentioned in Ron Brown's speech were substantial commercial concerns with global footprints who were expert at playing the Washington, DC game. Moments ago, I was glowing with self-satisfaction, and now this—public humiliation.

Only Secretary Brown was not quite finished: "But ladies and gentlemen, there is one US company that has done more than any other to showcase US inventiveness and build entrepreneurial bridges with our host country of Ghana . . . and that company is Omanhene."

Hallelujah.

Finally, someone publically recognized what we'd been trying so hard to accomplish here in Ghana. And not just anyone, but one of the most charismatic cabinet secretaries in modern US history. Secretary Brown, by all accounts, was a singular individual. He cared as passionately for a small business as he did for a global conglomerate. The man simply loved business, sympathized with underdogs, and relished the stories behind companies. I was later told by his staff that the Secretary served Omanhene on his flight over to Africa and regaled the official delegation with the saga of my company. Omanhene couldn't ask for a better champion.

Two weeks later, Ron Brown and several of his senior staff were killed in an airplane crash while on a trade mission to Dubrovnik.

* * *

I came to appreciate how "the little chocolate factory that could" storyline was useful to the governments of both Ghana and the United States. Ghana desperately wanted to demonstrate to a global audience that it did *something well*, that it was more than just a source of bauxite, gold, or cocoa. Ghana wanted to ascend the manufacturing

value chain and to craft upscale products. The US wanted to dispel the stereotype of the Ugly American, lacking any cross-cultural nuance, and to demonstrate that its economy consisted of smaller companies, too, not just consumer-product conglomerates seeking to enter virgin markets and displace local shopkeepers. There were moments when I felt that each country was—what is the word here—*exploiting* Omanhene rather than advancing the interests of the company. And yet, I confess, attention from either country (for whatever the reason) didn't hurt Omanhene's cause, either. Such is the give-and-take of any commercial exchange. We all need each other—and we use each other, too.

Back home, Omanhene continued to grow, adding new customers, including the Smithsonian Museum gift shop. I hired my first sales representatives, who secured a meeting with Starbucks. Based upon an initial product review, we were invited to hold a blind taste test of our hot chocolate at the Starbucks regional office in Chicago. At the tasting, about a dozen store managers sampled both the Starbucks house brand of hot cocoa and Omanhene. The results of the side-by-side taste test were impressive: every single manager selected Omanhene as the favorite. But a few weeks later, Starbucks executives decided to purchase their own cocoa processing facility, putting an end to talks of selling Omanhene in its cafés.

* * *

My seesaw existence continued: bad news, good news, often both at once. The US Commerce Department invited me to return to Accra and join a panel of US business executives, sharing insights and wisdom with African government leaders. The occasion was the annual meeting of developing economies that benefit from the African Growth and Opportunity Act, known as AGOA, a compilation of laws and regulatory incentives designed to promote bilateral trade among more than three dozen African countries and the US. Think of AGOA as NAFTA for Africa—only far less threatening to the US economy, since Africa produces so few manufactured goods that the displacement of US jobs is minimal, by comparison.

If you were an African trade minister, the subtext for this panel presentation might be titled "Things You Need to Change If You Hope to Attract US Business Investment." On the other hand, I wondered how many of the assembled ministers saw that the AGOA summit was also part of a US-composed counterpoint to the symphonic crescendo of Chinese expansionism in Africa.

Each panel member was allotted twenty minutes for individual remarks before the panel took questions from the floor. Tone was important. I didn't want to insult this audience of senior ministers and central bank officials, most of whom had MBAs and PhDs from the top universities in the world.

How to distill my thoughts on globalism? Taking the long view, it is axiomatic that international trade creates overall economic wealth, opens new markets, and promotes efficiency—the rational allocation of scarce resources—or so a mainstream economist would argue. Put less artfully, free trade allows US companies to sell outside the US market, a market that, despite its aggregate size, is no longer fast-growing. With modest population growth and a rising inequality of income, the US consumer market is unlikely to generate anything beyond incremental annual growth. Writ large, it's easy to argue that globalism, if practiced wisely, is a good thing for . . . *the globe*. Writ small, there are winners and losers. Think of US steel workers losing jobs to steel workers in India. Or consider the shoe industry, where manufacturing is now located primarily in Asia. Since all politics is local, trade issues become devilishly difficult for your average parliamentarian or congressperson. We all love affordable athletic shoes; so by extension, we all ought to support the notion of free trade, the framework that allows inexpensive shoes from abroad to enter local markets. But if you happen to live in a constituency with the last remaining shoe factory, say, in Vermont or Blackpool, and that company is being undersold by cheap imports and is now facing bankruptcy, then free trade is tantamount to economic ruin.

So, in this context, I understood that the Omanhene story is especially compelling. This panel presentation was not the first time I had found myself serving as a poster child for how globalism, if skillfully rendered, can result in benefits to both trading countries. I would bring a contrarian bilateral message, advocating for the necessity of granting African countries access to the lucrative US market and promoting the export of US ingenuity and creativity. I had a lot to say but not much time to say it. *I can do this*, I concluded hopefully—plus, I would share my "Twelve Rules for Dealing with Americans," a welcome respite, I hoped, from the quant-speak and business buzzword-laden speeches typical of these conferences—all in the allotted twenty minutes.

Wallace's Twelve Rules for Dealing with Americans

1. It's not how you dress, it's whether you show up on time. (Americans would rather be on time than catch a glimpse of the famed Ashanti Golden Stool.) Speak quickly and execute quickly.
2. Americans say they love free enterprise but secretly they want to be monopolists—and they behave that way.
3. The person at the top really does call all the shots.
4. There is nothing free about the free enterprise system. You get what you pay for (and don't get what you don't pay for). And so help me, you can't believe how much you really have to pay for. Often, intangibles such as credit information, legal counsel, market research, design expertise, and business advice are valuable commodities—you should expect to pay for everything.
5. The American who is dying to do a deal with you may well be the worst possible partner for you.

6. Your ideal American partner likely doesn't know you exist, can't find your country with two hands and a map, and has absolutely no interest in your product. It's your job to transform this ignorance.

7. Americans abhor meetings.

8. Not all American businesses are as rich as Croesus. Beware the company that promises you the world. No company can deliver the entire lucrative US market for free. Concentrate on your market segment. Your choices: price, service, and quality. Choose two.

9. Americans often want quality or perceived quality more than they want a cheap price. This places great importance on proper long-term (i.e., costly) brand management. If you execute this strategy properly, you will own a valuable brand name. Exploitation of a brand name—by means of intellectual property law—is one of the only ways you can legally operate as a monopolist in the US.

10. You don't have to own the whole US market to make money in the US. The most profitable firms often sell only to a tightly defined market niche. You should have a predilection for working with smaller businesses that are less likely to demand unreasonable terms in your business dealings.

11. Quality really is more important than quantity. Don't assume you need to devote all of your production to the US or let yourself be pushed into doing so.

12. Americans take things personally.

I would not share with the AGOA audience in Accra my "Seven Rules for Dealing with Ghanaians":

Wallace's Seven Rules for Dealing with Ghanaians

1. The managing director likely wears sandals, a short-sleeve shirt, and no tie; he will probably show up late with two cell

phones, and he will interrupt your meeting by taking outside calls. Don't mistake delay and interruptions for rudeness. Patience isn't merely a virtue; it's a necessity. Ghanaians view haste with suspicion.

2. Ghanaians hate monopolists and wouldn't want to be one even if they could. Note: Most Ghanaians work within a monopoly. When I first started Omanhene, the public sector comprised 85 percent of *all* jobs in the country.

3. The person at the top (or who you think is the top) doesn't likely call the shots. Titles matter a lot and seniority is firmly entrenched. Talent is infrequently rewarded. Often the deputy chief is the *real* power behind the title. A deputy can operate out of the public eye, while a minister or chief executive cannot.

4. Ghanaians love meetings. Indeed, they covet a "sitting allowance"—money paid for just showing up to board meetings.

5. Not all Ghanaians are financially poor (i.e., not every Ghanaian wants to do business with you on your terms). Consider: You're not doing them a favor by dealing with them—or are you?

6. When purchasing from Ghanaians, quantity is perceived to be more important than quality. Big numbers impress. Great big numbers impress greatly. Ghanaians think you want their entire production capacity. If you don't, what's wrong with you?

7. Ghanaians take things personally.

* * *

The AGOA conference was held at Accra's new International Exhibition Center, an aspirational cubist structure painted bright pink. It was, in the manner of many municipal convention centers, more pomp (or in this case *pouf*) than circumstance. On the afternoon before our presentation, the chair of our panel, the Deputy Administrator of the Small Business Administration (SBA), wanted to meet with the American contingent to go over the logistics. This was not surprising, considering she was a former UPS senior executive in charge of air operations, a charming, soft-spoken, political appointee. For all her Texas sweetness, however, the Deputy Administrator had a disarming "let's-keep-this-tight-we-represent-the-United-States-of-America" authoritativeness, the demeanor of a strict high school honors English teacher about to discourse on the bawdy parts of the *Decameron*. I liked her immediately.

Panelists and administrators alike, nearly a dozen of us, greeted one another briefly in the lobby and climbed three flights of stairs to find our designated meeting room. The door was locked. A key was eventually found. The sweltering room filled with serious people, cell phones un-holstered, clipboards, Day-Timers, and Filofaxes at the ready.

I reflected on how the US government is not unlike the British monarchy. The Queen has her equerries, ladies-in-waiting, subalterns of various sorts, as do Prince Philip, Prince Charles, Prince Andrew, and the lesser royals. The Deputy Administrator of the SBA had an assistant, a self-actualized twentysomething balancing a four-inch briefing binder on her lap—a binder in which the Deputy Administrator's bathroom breaks were presumably, and precisely, scheduled. Also present, the Assistant Secretary of Commerce for Africa, the Middle East, and Asia, who had her own assistant. The State Department had people "from post" (the US Embassy in Accra) and people from Washington, DC. All senior people had an assistant. Acronyms flew: USAID, TDA, PEPFAR, MCC, AGOA.

The Deputy Assistant's undersecretary (from Commerce, State, Treasury? I got confused) waved her hand in the direction of *her* assistant, like a choir director requesting pianissimo from the alto section. The assistant nodded knowingly but said nothing. The drama unfolded:

DEPUTY ADMINISTRATOR OF THE SBA:
If I can have everyone's attention for a moment.
Thank you. I want to review logistics for tomorrow. I
suggest that we take our places on stage as a group,
and then I'll introduce the first panel.

DEPUTY ADMINISTRATOR OF THE SBA'S
PERSONAL ASSISTANT:
*[Forever tugging at her skirt to better cover her
stockinged thighs]*
Excuse me, ma'am. Will you be at the podium or
speaking from the head table?

DEPUTY ADMINISTRATOR OF THE SBA:
I suppose I'll be sitting.

COMMISSAR FOR AFRICAN AID:
*[A man sporting a tonsure and wearing a short-sleeve
dress shirt]*
So, we all sit until you call us up to speak,
correct?

DEPUTY ADMINISTRATOR OF THE SBA:
Yes, of course. By the way, how many panelists do we
have?

ASSISTANT TO THE DEPUTY ADMINISTRATOR OF THE SBA'S
PERSONAL ASSISTANT:
Well, that's the thing . . . we have fifteen
scheduled, but three are missing.

DEPUTY ADMINISTRATOR OF THE SBA:
Fifteen?

[Rifling through her briefing binder]
I don't think they have fifteen chairs onstage.

UNDER-ASSISTANT:
Not at the head table, but I think there are chairs
behind the head table-not the head table chairs-but,
you know, a second row *behind the chairs* that are
behind the head table. In any case, we could add some
chairs back behind the table.

STATE DEPARTMENT SPECIAL ASSISTANT FOR PROTOCOL:
Can't go there. Ghana Protocol is responsible for the
chairs.
*[Silence, as the full weight and foreboding implications
of any involvement from Ghana Protocol is considered by
all in the room]*

DEPUTY ASSISTANT UNDERSECRETARY'S ASSISTANT:
Perhaps we sit with the audience in the front row?
And then, Madame Deputy Administrator, you can call
up each panel, one at a time . . .

DEPUTY ADMINISTRATOR OF THE SBA:
Fine. I'd like everyone, once you finish with
your speech, to move to the head table for the
Q&A. The previous panelists will file off prior
to this.

UNDER-ASSISTANT:
Ma'am, do you want the previous panelists to step
down one at a time or en masse?
*[More silence as the logistical pitfalls begin their
inexorable cascade. The young Under-Assistant mistakenly*

*thinks it is her use of French that has prompted the
awkward silence]*

That is, er . . . in a group?

[It goes on like this, so help me, for an hour]

DEPUTY ADMINISTRATOR OF THE SBA NURSE RATCHED:
Mr. Wallace, are you okay?

STEVE WALLACE:
*[Daubing eyes with a paper napkin, tears running freely
down his cheeks . . .]*

Just a dust mote in my eye . . .
*[Embarrassingly loud throat-clearing to mask spasms of
laughter . . .]*

FIRST COMMERCIAL OFFICER, US EMBASSY-ACCRA:
[Whispering to aide]

Who is this guy again?

STEVE WALLACE:
I suggest, for what it's worth, that we just sort of
play it by ear. Because, whatever we decide, you can
  pretty much bet that the Government of Ghana will
change things at the last possible minute, and we'll
be right back to where we started this meeting . . .
[Wallace glances at his wristwatch for dramatic effect]
. . . an hour ago.
[Agonizing silence]

It's just a thought, really . . .

DEPUTY ADMINISTRATOR OF THE SBA NURSE RATCHED:
Why, that's an *excellent* suggestion, Steven.

Secretly, deep down inside, I swelled with pride.

* * *

On the day of the big speech, I arrived at the Pink Palace at 7:30 a.m., over an hour early, as I needed to print out a reading copy of my speech. But I'd already been up for hours. To save money, I stayed at the Sunrise Hotel, a modest, locally owned hostel, instead of the official AGOA conference hotel, part of a multinational hospitality chain, where nearly every American visiting Ghana now stays. The business center at the Sunrise was cleverly called the "Brain Box," but no one could figure out how to send a copy of my speech to the Brain Box printer. An earnest front desk clerk offered to print the speech on the hotel's computer.

"Please, sir. I shall go and come," he said brightly, taking my writeable CD and repairing to a back room. He returned in a few moments with my printout, CD, and a forlorn look on his face. "Sir, I beg of you. Please, our printer cartridge is running *too* low on toner. Ah-haaaah."

The hard copy of my speech was unreadable, so badly streaked that it looked like a Giacometti monoprint. "How do you say *verkakte* in Twi?"

"Please? I beg your pardon, sir?"

I decided to go straight to the International Exhibition Center and see whether I'd have better luck there. Inside the lobby, the claustrophobia that beset me at the exact time I started Omanhene—a manifestation, I'm certain, of nagging economic insecurity and loss of control—caused a frisson of fear. I bypassed the elevator and climbed three flights of stairs to the conveniently located US Government Control Center, a special room where State Department staff furiously surfed the net, read e-mails, and studied memoranda and communiqués. There were several open computer terminals for the use of official guests, and I assumed that included me, since I was an invited speaker. In any case, no one thought to ask for my credentials. I sat down and was grateful that a neatly printed label on the monitor informed me that the log-on username was "Username" and the password was "Password." After successfully printing my speech and reviewing my remarks, I allowed myself a rare bit of self-satisfaction—I was pleased with what I'd written. I headed back down the three flights of stairs to the VIP holding pen to await my entrance.

Yes, I was happy with my speech. I looked at it again. *Speech?* At five minutes, my speech barely qualified as "brief remarks." I was working on it until 1:00 a.m., paring it down from its original twenty to just five minutes in length, as Ghana Protocol had insisted on adding various last-minute speakers to the agenda, and ordered the US participants to trim their presentations accordingly.

The plenary was supposed to start at 8:30 a.m., but the plenary chair, Ghana's Minister of Trade and Industry, Moses Atta-Marfo, arrived fully forty-five minutes late *for the second day in a row*. It took another half-hour to begin, as there seemed to be some further heated discussions amongst the respective staffs of the US delegation and the Government of Ghana.

During this delay, the Deputy Administrator of the SBA wanted to review quickly the choreography for this morning's performance. I pushed through the mismatched chairs, confidently taking a seat in the innermost ring—as if this were a favorite undergraduate seminar, *Current Topics in Recombinant Fiction and Pataphysics*. I searched for a welcoming face amongst my fellow presenters. I saw none.

Our little theatrical continued:

DEPUTY ADMINISTRATOR OF THE SBA:
Thank you for your attention. Once the Minister
introduces me, we all file up onstage and take our
seats.

215

SPECIAL ASSISTANT FOR TRADE:
As a group or one at a time?

DEPUTY ADMINISTRATOR OF THE SBA:
By the way, I will do a greeting on behalf of the
whole group, "Honorable Minister, Deputy Secretary,
your Excellencies, and Honored Guests."

SPECIAL ASSISTANT FOR TRADE:
Madam Administrator, I beg your pardon, you should
add, "All Protocols Preserved." It means that if
you forgot someone's title, it is presumed to be
included.

I rose on the pretense of having to use the bathroom; I grimaced and patted my stomach, reprising my long-running Sunyani mime performance, only this time it was to hide the fact that I had developed another ill-timed fit of laughter.

Even with such a late start, the convention hall filled up slowly, the audience no doubt having taken its cue from the late start the previous day. I was embarrassed for the Government of Ghana and upset that they had squandered this opportunity to dispel the stereotype that everything in West Africa runs woefully behind schedule. Many of the Government of Ghana junior staff—including Ghana Protocol—felt likewise; I could see it in their pained expressions. It was as if punctuality were the single most important thing they could do to demonstrate to the world that, here in Ghana, despite our many challenges and shortcomings, *we start on time*. And they likely would have, but for one rogue minister with his own political agenda. Ghana was poised for success. So very, very close. Alas.

And so, the attendees—senior ministers from across the entire continent—assumed it no longer made sense to get up early just to hear Mr. Steven Wallace of Milwaukee, Wisconsin, share his learned reflections on African economic development.

Minister Atta-Marfo, who could barely conceal his own presidential ambitions, decided just that morning to add two Ghanaian investment bankers—probably big donors to his campaign—as a prelude to our panel. This rogue decision upset many:

1. The US State Department, which had worked on the AGOA agenda for fully eleven months and did not do well with last-minute surprises—they did not do well, *at-TAAAALL*!

2. The delegations from the more than three dozen other African countries, who themselves were jockeying for representation on these high-profile panels, regarded this eleventh-hour addition as "stacking the deck" unfairly in favor of host country Ghana.

3. The Deputy Administrator of the SBA, who expected this panel, like her dozens of 747 jumbo jets, tens of thousands of UPS trucks, and a hundred thousand bandy-legged UPS drivers wearing brown shorts and matching knee socks, to *run on time and keep to the effing schedule, goddammit!*

It got worse. The two investment bankers were nowhere to be found; they were apparently stuck in Accra's notorious traffic. Instead of moving on to the next speakers on the agenda—we were now fully two hours behind schedule—Minister Atta-Marfo decided incredibly, inexplicably, *to wait until the bankers arrived.* To fill the time, the Minister sidled up to the podium and spoke extemporaneously on the basics of project finance, an introductory-level lecture that fell embarrassingly flat before an audience comprised of trade and finance ministers, most of whom were educated at Harvard Business School, Wharton, or the London School of Economics. I whispered to my seatmate that someone should remind the Minister that the delegations of the thirty-six other African countries *are not eligible to vote in Ghana's upcoming presidential elections*, so the impromptu campaign speech was unnecessary. Our panel chair, Madam UPS Secretary, must have been livid, but she was the consummate diplomat and betrayed nothing.

My turn finally arrived. I made my way to the lectern, wondering how, in just five minutes, it was possible to make a favorable impression on this weary audience, subjected to two long days of bloviating. Best, I decided, to grab their attention. Without saying a word, I plunked down a tin of Omanhene hot cocoa and then, by contrast, carefully placed one of our deluxe gift boxes on the lectern, taking my time to adjust the angle so the full logo was in view. The audience seemed puzzled. They were wondering why I hadn't started to speak, why I was futzing with box and tin, my impromptu product placement. Finally, I turned my attention away from my products, looked up, and smiled broadly to the audience.

"Always be selling," I quipped, deploying my favorite line from the play *Glengarry Glen Ross*.

For the first time in two days, laughter filled the hall.

Victory!

Thank you, David Mamet.

* * *

I woke up early the morning after my speech. There was no electricity. No phone service. No air conditioning. As satisfying as it was to speak at the AGOA event, and to have marshaled high-level US government advocacy, I realized that my situation was dire. At the exact moment when I was ramping up sales, I might find myself without production capacity—a catastrophic outcome. I did a quick accounting. I totted up my victories: I'd survived threatened legal action over our flagship gift box, won an international design award for the selfsame gift box, secured sales from Japan to the

Smithsonian Museum, and found a way to impress Starbucks store managers in a blind taste test. But I also had to tally losses in my ledger: Commerce Secretary Ron Brown was no more, V.S. Hope & Company was no more, Joseph Bonsu-Mensah was under investigation, and MacFinn wanted no more to do with me. The Omanhene factory was in limbo, awaiting a divestiture that only the World Bank seemed to welcome.

I had clambered far out on a limb and could feel the bough beginning to sway. I had run out of options.

Wənna a, wənso dae.
If one does not slumber, one cannot dream.

*"If the circumstance does not call for a proverb,
do not use one."*

CHAPTER 16

Back to the Basement

Winter, 1997. The irony of my situation weighed on me. Most companies struggle to find customers and to generate sales. The most expensive and vexing challenge of any business is nearly always customer acquisition and retention. It's no wonder that an active customer base is often the most highly valued of any company asset. By comparison, making chocolate is relatively easy, especially if you are provided with the recipes, the brand name, and the package design, and if you receive payment in advance via an irrevocable letter of credit. *Thank you, Omanhene.* I had hoped that our contributions to this effort would be properly valued, or at least better recognized, by my Ghanaian partners.

For decades, Ghana had wanted to move up the cocoa value chain. They coveted the profits that accrued to European chocolatiers. Economic theory going back to David Ricardo provided a road map. Ghana grows some of the finest cocoa in the world. Ghana *owns* a freshness advantage—a comparative advantage—that no other European or North American chocolate-making country can match. And yet for decades Ghana failed to secure any sustained exports from their own timid attempts to produce finished chocolate. They failed in their effort to produce a product that customers wanted to buy. And then, out of the blue, I not only brought them first-world customers, but I paid Ghana in hard currency, US dollars. I did all of this for free; it hadn't cost Portem or the Ghana Cocoa Board a single pesewa. To my view, Omanhene had done all the heavy lifting.

I'd presented Portem with the most elusive asset of any business: repeat customers. All I needed was for Ghana simply to make Omanhene chocolate according to our recipe, and on a production schedule that served our growing customer base.

To be sure, there were other things I would like Ghana to do. We could secure faster growth, for instance, if we could work together even more robustly, more strategically. Ultimately, though, the Omanhene enterprise itself had provided the missing link, solved the million-dollar question—a question that stretched back to the old TDA Pre-feasibility Study: Would Ghana be able to produce gourmet chocolate worthy of export markets?

The answer remained muddled. Yes, Ghana could manufacture fine chocolate but, for today, on its own, Ghana was unable to *acquire and retain customers for its chocolate*. For better or worse, Omanhene needed Portem, and Portem needed Omanhene.

I can't really blame Ghana—for generations, the country never needed to develop marketing or sales skills; the old Gold Coast inhabitants almost certainly never articulated a value proposition or cultivated customers—they didn't need to. Western colonial powers simply appeared, as if by magic, paid for local labor, and took what they wanted. Ghana's colonial history reduced the country to a nation that sold its patrimony to foreign off-takers rather than to true customers. There's an enormous difference. Off-takers dictate the price, they appear when the commodity conditions are favorable, and they depart the moment commodity conditions turn sour. By contrast, customers must be pursued and romanced, requiring all the elements that go into stating a value proposition (quality, service, durability, reliability, performance, price)—and if properly cultivated, customers will pay a premium for products and services such that you earn their loyalty over time.

This lack of sales and marketing expertise is even more paradoxical because—and allow me to paint with a very broad brush here—Ghana is a nation brimming with what the Akan call the *akwaaba* spirit of hospitality, generosity, humor, and warmth. Yet, in so many business situations in modern Ghana, customer service skills are surprisingly low—at odds with the innate amicability of most Ghanaians. Why? Perhaps it is because for generations, colonial powers simply took all of Ghana's cocoa, rubber, gold, and diamonds; hence, Ghana never needed to develop the soft skills necessary to entice and solicit customers. It seems like such a waste of Ghana's most valuable natural resource: its people.

One morning at three o'clock, I got a phone call from Joe Bimpong, the new head of Ghana's Divestiture Implementation Committee. "Steven? No divestiture will take place," he said.

Sleepy, I found it hard to comprehend what he said. Even as he went on, I struggled to process the very first thing out of his mouth. Divestiture, Joe suggested, was never really a serious possibility. The World Bank's "conditionalities" notwithstanding, the Government of Ghana would never dream of relinquishing an asset as valuable as its first cocoa-processing factory.

I was stunned. So, the outcome—after all the time, energy, effort, money, and anxiety I put into this—was *no change at all*? I was right back where I started?

Joe must have guessed how his news affected me. At last he paused, and then, with audible insouciance, he said, "Ei, this is Ghana, Steven."

Just what did he mean, *"This is Ghana?"* That Ghana perennially finds a way to get what it wants from the donor/creditor community? That Ghana has perfected the fine art of inaction, happy to wallow in its tropical inertia? That the state apparatus windmills furiously without having to accept change, embrace something new, or risk anything *at-TALL*?

Or perhaps Joe Bimpong was saying that Ghana—perhaps life, really—is one long frustration, a slow, smoldering burn, a supreme test of endurance and one not to be taken *too* seriously, lest you wilt in the torpor of the Mampong Hills.

I hung up the phone. The call had awakened my infant son, Ben, and I tiptoed back to his room, rocking him desperately before he woke my wife. Tucking him back in his crib, I crept down to the basement as quietly as possible.

For the rest of the night, I would be hard at work: hand-filling, sealing, and labeling tins of Omanhene hot cocoa mix. The corporate lights would burn steadily, if not brightly. The Omanhene ship of state would sail on, listing only slightly, as it steamed toward its uncertain future.

Twenty years later, I'm still in business.

Wo pusu nunum a, na wo te ne kankan
If you shake the aromatic "nunum" bush, you perceive it's scent.

"The only way to know a person's true character
is to actually test them."